The Collected Later Poems

By William Carlos Williams

† *City Lights Books*

The Collected Later Poems of

WILLIAM
CARLOS
WILLIAMS

Revised Edition

A NEW DIRECTIONS BOOK

Revised Edition
Book Design by Maurice Serle Kaplan
Manufactured in the United States of America

New Directions Books are published for James Laughlin
by New Directions Publishing Corporation,
80 Eighth Avenue, New York 10011

EIGHTH PRINTING

To James Laughlin

Contents

Acknowledgements

Some of the poems in this volume were first printed in the following magazines: Arizona Quarterly, Botteghe Oscure, Briarcliff Quarterly, Calendar, Contemporary Poetry, Cronos, Fantasy, Furioso, General Magazine (U. of P.), Harper's Bazaar, Harvard Wake, Hemispheres, Kenyon Review, The Nation, New Directions, The New Leader, New Poems 1940, The New Republic, The New Yorker, Palisade, Partisan Review, The Poet of the Year, Poetry, A Magazine of Verse, Poets at Work, The Quarterly Review of Literature, The Tiger's Eye, View, VVV, Yale Poetry Review, and Zero. Eleven poems were published by Richard Wirtz Emerson and Frederick Eckman in 1949 as Golden Goose Chap Book I, entitled *The Pink Church*.

The Wedge

Author's Introduction (1944)

THE WAR is the first and only thing in the world today.

The arts generally are not, nor is this writing a diversion from that for relief, a turning away. It is the war or part of it, merely a different sector of the field.

Critics of rather better than average standing have said in recent years that after socialism has been achieved it's likely there will be no further use for poetry, that it will disappear. This comes from nothing else than a faulty definition of poetry—and the arts generally. I don't hear anyone say that mathematics is likely to be outmoded, to disappear shortly. Then why poetry?

It is an error attributable to the Freudian concept of the thing, that the arts are a resort from frustration, a misconception still entertained in many minds.

They speak as though action itself in all its phases were not compatible with frustration. All action the same. But Richard Coeur de Lion wrote at least one of the finest lyrics of his day. Take Don Juan for instance. Who isn't frustrated and does not prove it by his actions—if you want to say so?

But through art the psychologically maimed may become the most distinguished man of his age. Take Freud for instance.

The making of poetry is no more an evidence of frustration than is the work of Henry Kaiser or Timoshenko. It's the war, the driving forward of desire to a complex end. And when that shall have been achieved, mathematics and the arts will turn elsewhere—beyond the atom if necessary for their reward and let's all be frustrated together.

A man isn't a block that remains stationary though the psychologists treat him so—and most take an insane pride in believing it. Consistency! He varies; Hamlet today, Caesar tomorrow; here, there, somewhere—if he is to retain his sanity, and why not?

The arts have a complex relation to society. The poet isn't a fixed phenomenon, no more is his work. That might be a note on current affairs, a diagnosis, a plan for procedure, a retrospect—all in its own peculiarly enduring form. There need be nothing limited or frustrated about that. It may be a throw-off from the most violent and successful action or run parallel to it, a saga. It may be the picking out of an essential detail for memory, something to be set aside for further study, a sort of shorthand of emotional significances for later reference.

Let the metaphysical take care of itself, the arts have nothing to do with it. They will concern themselves with it if they please, among other things.

To make two bald statements: There's nothing sentimental about a machine, and: A poem is a small (or large) machine made of words. When I say there's nothing sentimental about a poem I mean that there can be no part, as in any other machine, that is redundant.

Prose may carry a load of ill-defined matters like a ship. But poetry is the machine which drives it, pruned to a perfect economy. As in all machines its movement is intrinsic, undulant, a physical more than a literary character. In a poem this movement is distinguished in each case by the character of the speech from which it arises.

Therefore each speech having its own character the poetry it engenders will be peculiar to that speech also in its own intrinsic form. The effect is beauty, what in a single object resolves our complex feelings of propriety. One doesn't seek beauty. All that an artist or a Sperry can do is to drive toward his purpose, in the nature of his materials; not to take gold where Babbitt metal is called for; to make: make clear the complexity of his perceptions in the medium given to him by inheritance, chance, accident or whatever it may be to work with according to his talents and the will that drives them. Don't talk about frustration fathering the arts. The bastardization of words is too widespread for that today.

My own interest in the arts has been extracurricular. Up from the gutter, so to speak. Of necessity. Each age and place to its own. But in the U. S. the necessity for recognizing this intrinsic character has been largely ignored by the various English Departments of the academies.

When a man makes a poem, makes it, mind you, he takes words as he finds them interrelated about him and composes them—without distortion which would mar their exact significances—into an intense expression of his perceptions and ardors that they may constitute a revelation in the speech that he uses. It isn't what he says that counts as a work of art, it's what he makes, with such intensity of perception that it lives with an intrinsic movement of its own to verify its authenticity. Your attention is called now and then to some beautiful line or sonnet-sequence because of what is said there. So be it. To me all sonnets say the same thing of no importance. What does it matter what the line "says"?

There is no poetry of distinction without formal invention, for it is in the intimate form that works of art achieve their exact meaning, in which they most resemble the machine, to give language its highest dignity, its illumination in the environment to which it is native. Such war, as the arts live and breathe by, is continuous.

It may be that my interests as expressed here are pre-art. If so I look for a development along these lines and will be satisfied with nothing else.

A Sort of a Song

Let the snake wait under
his weed
and the writing
be of words, slow and quick, sharp
to strike, quiet to wait,
sleepless.

—through metaphor to reconcile
the people and the stones.
Compose. (No ideas
but in things) Invent!
Saxifrage is my flower that splits
the rocks.

Catastrophic Birth

Fury and counter fury! The volcano!
Stand firm, unbending. The chemistry
shifts. The retort does not fracture.
The change reveals—change.
The revelation is compact—
compact of regathered fury

By violence lost, recaptured by violence
violence alone opens the shell of the nut.
The best is hard to say—unless
near the break. Unless the shell hold
the kernel is not sweet.
Under violence the meat lies regained

Each age brings new calls upon violence
for new rewards, variants of the old.
Unless each hold firm
Unless each remain inflexible
there can be no new. The new opens
new ways beyond all known ways.

Shut up! laughs the big she-Wop.
Wait till you have six like a me.
Every year one. Come on! Push! Sure,
you said it! Maybe I have one next year.
Sweating like a volcano. It cleans you up,
makes you feel good inside. Come on! Push!

The impasse becomes a door when the wall
is levelled. The cone lifts, lifts
and settles back. Life goes on. The cone
blocks the crater and lifts half its height.
Life goes on. The orange trees bloom.
The old women talk tirelessly.

The laboratory announces officially
that there is no need to worry. The
cone is subsiding, smoke rises as
a funnel into the blue unnatural sky—
The change impends! A change stutters
in the rocks. We believe nothing can change.

The fracture will come, the death dealing
chemistry cannot be long held back.
The dreaded eruption blocks out the valley,
the careful prognosticator as well as
the idlers. The revelation is complete.
Peace is reborn above the cinders

Only one man is left, the drunkard
who had been confined underground to
rot with the rats and lizards.
The old woman who had been combing out
the child's hair is also intact
but at a touch she falls into a heap of ashes

Only he who had been confined
in disgrace underground is rescued alive
and he knows nothing more of it
than to stand and curse the authorities
who left him there so long without food
and liquor while they were digging him out

Rain will fall. The wind and the birds
will bring seeds, the river changes
its channel and fish re-enter it.
The seawind will come in from the east.
The broken cone breathes softly on
the edge of the sky, violence revives and
    regathers.

Paterson: the Falls

What common language to unravel?
The Falls, combed into straight lines
from that rafter of a rock's
lip. Strike in! the middle of

some trenchant phrase, some
well packed clause. Then . . .
This is my plan. 4 sections: First,
the archaic persons of the drama.

An eternity of bird and bush,
resolved. An unraveling:
the confused streams aligned, side
by side, speaking! Sound

married to strength, a strength
of falling—from a height! The wild
voice of the shirt-sleeved
Evangelist rivaling, Hear

me! I am the Resurrection
and the Life! echoing
among the bass and pickerel, slim
eels from Barbados, Sargasso

Sea, working up the coast to that
bounty, ponds and wild streams—
Third, the old town: Alexander Hamilton
working up from St. Croix,

from that sea! and a deeper, whence
he came! stopped cold

by that unmoving roar, fastened
there: the rocks silent

but the water, married to the stone,
voluble, though frozen; the water
even when and though frozen
still whispers and moans—

And in the brittle air
a factory bell clangs, at dawn, and
snow whines under their feet. Fourth,
the modern town, a

disembodied roar! the cataract and
its clamor broken apart—and from
all learning, the empty
ear struck from within, roaring . . .

The Dance

In Brueghel's great picture, The Kermess,
the dancers go round, they go round and
around, the squeal and the blare and the
tweedle of bagpipes, a bugle and fiddles
tipping their bellies (round as the thick-
sided glasses whose wash they impound)
their hips and their bellies off balance
to turn them. Kicking and rolling about
the Fair Grounds, swinging their butts, those
shanks must be sound to bear up under such
rollicking measures, prance as they dance
in Breughel's great picture, The Kermess.

Writer's Prologue to a Play in Verse

In your minds you jump from doors
to sad departings, pigeons, dreams
of terror, to cathedrals; bowed,
repelled, knees quaking, to the-closed-
without-a-key or through an arch
an ocean that races full of sound
and foam to lay a carpet for
your pleasure or a wood that waves
releasing hawks and crows or
crowds that elbow and fight for
a place or anything. You see it
in your minds and the mind at once
jostles it, turns it about, examines
and arranges it to suit its fancy.
Or rather changes it after a pattern
which is the mind itself, turning
and twisting the theme until it gets
a meaning or finds no meaning and
is dropped. By such composition,
without code, the scenes we see move
and, as it may happen, make
a music, a poetry
which the poor poet copies if
and only if he is able—to astonish
and amuse, for your delights,
in public, face to face with you
individually and secretly addressed.

We are not here, you understand,
but in the mind, that circumstance
of which the speech is poetry.
Then look, I beg of you, try and
look within yourselves rather than

at me for what I shall discover.
Yourselves! Within yourselves. Tell
me if you do not see there, alive!
a creature unlike the others, something
extraordinary in its vulgarity,
something strange, unnatural to
the world, that suffers the world poorly,
is tripped at home, disciplined at
the office, greedily eats money—
for a purpose: to escape the tyranny
of lies. And is all they can think
of to amuse you, a ball game? Or
skiing in Van Diemen's land in August
—to amuse you! Do you not come here
to escape that? For you are merely
distracted, not relieved in the blood,
deadened, defeated, stultified.
But this! is new. Believe it, to be
proved presently by your patience.
Run through the public appearance
of it, to come out—not stripped
but, if you'll pardon me, something
which in the mind you are and would
be yet have always been, unrecognized,
tragic and foolish, without a tongue.
That's it. Yourself the thing
you are, speechless—because there is
no language for it, shockingly revealed.

Would it disturb you if I said
you have no other speech than poetry?
You, yourself, I mean. There is
no other language for it than the poem
—falsified by the critics until
you think it's something else, fight
it off, as idle, a kind of lie,

smelling of corpses, that the practical
world rejects. How could it be you?
Never! without invention. It is, if
you'll have patience, the undiscovered
language of yourself, which you avoid,
rich and poor, killed and killers,
a language to be coaxed out of poets—
possibly, an intolerable language
that will frighten—to which
you are not used. We must make it
easy for you, feed it to you slowly
until you let down the barriers,
relax before it. But it's easy
if you will allow me to proceed, it
can make transformations, give it
leave to do its work in you.

Accept the convention as you would
opera, provisionally; let me go ahead.
Wait to see if the revelation
happen. It may not.
Or it may come and go, small bits
at a time. But even the chips of it
are invaluable. Wait to learn
the hang of its persuasions as it makes
its transformations from the common
to the undisclosed and lays that open
where—you will see a frightened face!

But believe! that poetry will be
in the terms you know, insist on that
and can and must break through everything,
all the outward forms, to re-dress
itself humbly in that which you
yourself will say is the truth, the
exceptional truth of ordinary people,
14   the extraordinary truth. You shall see.

It isn't masculine more than it is
feminine, it's not a book more than
it is speech; inside the mind, natural
to the mind as metals are to rock,
a gist, puppets which if they present
distinction it is from that hidden
dignity which they, by your leave,
reflect from you who are the play.

This is a play of a husband and a wife.
As you love your husband or your wife
or if you hate him or if you hate
her, watch the language! see if you
think that it expresses something of
the things, to your knowledge, that
take place in the mind and in the world
but seldom on the lips. This play
is of a woman and her lover, all
mixed up, of life and death and all
the secret language that runs through
those curious transactions, seldom
heard but in the deadest presentations
now respectfully unnaturalized.

For pleasure! pleasure, not for
cruelty but to make you laugh, until
you cry like General Washington
at the river. Seeing the travellers
bathing there who had had their clothes
stolen, how he laughed! And how
you shall laugh to see yourselves
all naked, on the stage!

Burning the Christmas Greens

Their time past, pulled down
cracked and flung to the fire
—go up in a roar

All recognition lost, burnt clean
clean in the flame, the green
dispersed, a living red,
flame red, red as blood wakes
on the ash—

and ebbs to a steady burning
the rekindled bed become
a landscape of flame

At the winter's midnight
we went to the trees, the coarse
holly, the balsam and
the hemlock for their green

At the thick of the dark
the moment of the cold's
deepest plunge we brought branches
cut from the green trees

to fill our need, and over
doorways, about paper Christmas
bells covered with tinfoil
and fastened by red ribbons

we stuck the green prongs
in the windows hung
woven wreaths and above pictures
the living green. On the

mantle we built a green forest
and among those hemlock
sprays put a herd of small
white deer as if they

were walking there. All this!
and it seemed gentle and good
to us. Their time past,
relief! The room bare. We

stuffed the dead grate
with them upon the half burnt out
log's smoldering eye, opening
red and closing under them

and we stood there looking down.
Green is a solace
a promise of peace, a fort
against the cold (though we

did not say so) a challenge
above the snow's
hard shell. Green (we might
have said) that, where

small birds hide and dodge
and lift their plaintive
rallying cries, blocks for them
and knocks down

the unseeing bullets of
the storm. Green spruce boughs
pulled down by a weight of
snow—Transformed!

Violence leaped and appeared.
Recreant! roared to life
as the flame rose through and
our eyes recoiled from it.

In the jagged flames green
to red, instant and alive. Green!
those sure abutments . . . Gone!
lost to mind

and quick in the contracting
tunnel of the grate
appeared a world! Black
mountains, black and red—as

yet uncolored—and ash white,
an infant landscape of shimmering
ash and flame and we, in
that instant, lost,

breathless to be witnesses,
as if we stood
ourselves refreshed among
the shining fauna of that fire.

In Chains

When blackguards and murderers
under cover of their offices
accuse the world of those villainies
which they themselves invent to
torture us—we have no choice
but to bend to their designs,
buck them or be trampled while
our thoughts gnaw, snap and bite
within us helplessly—unless
we learn from that to avoid
being as they are, how love
will rise out of its ashes if
we water it, tie up the slender
stem and keep the image of its
lively flower chiseled upon our minds.

In Sisterly Fashion

The ugly woman clutched
her lover round the neck
her skin was white as snow
as she wept softly to herself
knowing her lack of beauty
like the sting of death—
by which she praised in
sisterly fashion your fitted
limbs your honied breath

The World Narrowed to a Point

Liquor and love
when the mind is dull
focus the wit
on a world of form

The eye awakes
perfumes are defined
inflections
ride the quick ear

Liquor and love
rescue the cloudy sense
banish its despair
give it a home.

The Observer

What a scurvy mind
whose constant breath
still simulates
the forms of death—
unable or unwilling
to own the common
things which we must
do to live again
and be in love and
all its quickening
pleasures prove—

A Flowing River

You are lovely as a river
under tranquil skies—
There are imperfections
but a music overlays them—

telling by how dark a bed
the current moves
to what sea that shines
and ripples in my thought

The Hounded Lovers

Where shall we go?
Where shall we go
    who are in love?

Juliet went
to Friar Laurence's cell
    but we have no rest—

Rainwater lies on
the hard ground reflecting
    the morning sky

But where shall we go?
We cannot resolve ourselves
    into a dew

nor sink into the earth.
Shall we postpone it
    to Eternity?

The dry heads of the
goldenrod
    turned to stiff ghosts

jerk at their stalks
signaling grave warning.
    Where shall we go?

The movement of benediction
does not turn back
    the cold wind.

The Cure

Sometimes I envy others, fear them
a little too, if they write well.
For when I cannot write I'm a sick man
and want to die. The cause is plain.

But they have no access to my sources.
Let them write then as they may and
perfect it as they can they will never
come to the secret of that form

interknit with the unfathomable ground
where we walk daily and from which
among the rest you have sprung
and opened flower-like to my hand.

To All Gentleness

Like a cylindrical tank fresh silvered
upended on the sidewalk to advertise
some plumber's shop, a profusion
of pink roses bending ragged in the rain—
speaks to me of all gentleness and its
enduring.

        Secure in the enclosing rain,
a column of tears borne up by the heavy
flowers: the new and the unlikely, bound
indissolubly together in one mastery.

Out of fear lest the flower be broken
the rose puts out its thorns. That
is the natural way.

        We witless, wistful
of the flower, unable still by heavy
emphasis to praise enough its silence,
inventors of opera as national background;
the classic tradition, bellowing
masks, long since decayed, in our time
also perishes.

        And they speak,
euphemistically, of the anti-poetic!
Garbage. Half the world ignored . . .

Is this praise of gentleness?

        The lion
according to old paintings will
lie down with the lamb. But what is meant

has not been precisely enough stated:
missed or—postponed.
The arrow! That the arrow fly!

Forthwith she holds it to the string, the
hygienic arrow! that, crescent, she
may achieve poise, win perhaps a prize
later at the meet or making a profession
of it grow to be a teacher of the art

—and the innocent shaft, released,
plunges forward . . .

              The courts are
overcrowded, fear obsesses all intimacies
unless legalized—and money,
articulated to government mounts still
as wonder in the minds of the speculators,

to buy
          (the ferment wedging their skulls
ever wider)

          to buy, shall we say, the
grass, or a small cloud perhaps (in
whose shadow a lifting wind whirls) or
if Queen Blanche, a pond
of waterlilies or the rain itself.

The natural way, to buy!

                —to buy off.

But if the wing of a plane in combat,
coming down, an uncertain landing, if

by the shattering prop of a plane he
is knocked into the sea,

gives himself up injured for lost and then—
his wound eased by the seawater—goes
on out of habit, swims alone among
the enquiring waves twelve hours, fourteen
hours. . . . picked up and
returned to this life.

That too is
the natural way, by claw and law—

To which
we are opposed!

For most
fear gentleness and misinterpret it,
which if by chance they meet the
longer arc, upgrade or downgrade, the
wash and swing, they are discomfited—

A matter of indifference—

the wave
rising or the wave curving to the hollow:

Swam hour after hour, the healthy
life he'd lead formerly at Seattle holding
him . . .

Or was it? Who
can tell? come back for all that a
month later when they'd released him held
incommunicado at the hospital, to say,
Here I am, as I promised!

                              Copernicus,
Shostakowitch. Is it the occasion
or the man? Take an apple and split it
between the thumbs. Which is which?

Caught in the shuffling of the wider
undulations one is brought down, another
lifted by the wash; a rush of algae
proliferant or a mammoth caught in the ice
hair and all for dogs later to dig
and devour . . .

            the phase, is supreme!

                    except
for gentleness that joins our lives
in one.

        But shoot! shoot straight,
they say. The arrow flies! the barb
is driven home and . . . strength
thrust upon weakness, the convulsive ecstasy

achieved, in the moment of impact
we are left deafened and blinded, blind to
the sun and moon, the brilliant
moonlight leaves, to fish and fowl:

                              the
bird in white above the swimming bird
and from the depths of the wood
the song that is the bird, unseen.

The bomb-sight adjusted destruction hangs
by a hair over the cities. Bombs away!

and the packed word descends—and
rightly so.

              The arrow! the arrow!

Only . . . that is . . .

the moment is lost! without us, the
completion, the learned moment. The gates
opened, it also falls away,
                    unrecognized!

It is, yes Jakus, the prize, the prize!
in which that which has been held from you,
my perky lad, is hid.

                The flower is our sign.

Milkweed, a single stalk on the bare
embankment (and where
does the imagination begin?

                  Violence and
gentleness, which is the core? Is
gentleness the core?)

              Slender green
reaching up from sand and rubble (the
anti-poetic they say ignorantly, a
disassociation)

            premising the flower,
without which, no flower.

              She was
forewoman to a gang at the ship foundry,

cleared the finished parts to
the loading platform; had three misses,
all boys, by the man she lives with—
and may the fourth be a boy also for which
he married her.

Tough, huh?

Never had a backache.

Not the girth of thigh, but
that gentleness that harbors all violence,
the valid juxtaposition, one
by the other, alternates, the cosine, the
cylinder and the rose.

Three Sonnets

As the eye lifts, the field
is moving—the river,
slowly between the stones
steadily under the bare
branches, heavy slabs close
packed with jagged rim-cupped
edges, seaward—

what was the mudbank
crowded, sparkling
with diamonds big as fists,
unbelievable to witness

The silent and snowy mountains
do not change their
poise—the broken line,
the mass whose darkness
meets the rising sun, waken
uncompromised above the gulls
upon the ice-strewn
river.

You cannot succor me,
you cannot change. I will
open my eyes at morning even though
their lids be sealed
faster by ice than stone!

3

My adored wife, this—in spite
of Dr. Kennedy's remark
that the story of the repeated
injury would sound bad in a divorce
court—the bastard:

In the one woman
I find all the rest—or nothing
and raise them thence and celebrate
them there and close their eyes
and bury them in her and
decorate their graves. Upon her
their memory clings, each one
distinct, enriching her
while I yet live to enjoy, perhaps.

St. Valentine

A woman's breasts
for beauty
A man's delights
for charm

The rod and cups
of duty
to stave us
from harm!

A woman's eyes
a woman's
thighs and a man's
straight look:

Cities rotted to
pig-sties
will stand up by
that book!

The Young Cat and the Chrysanthemums

You mince, you start
advancing indirectly—
your tail upright
knocking about among the
frail, heavily flowered
sprays.

Yes, you are lovely
with your ingratiating
manners, sleek sides and
small white paws but
I wish you had not come
here.

The Poem

It's all in
the sound. A song.
Seldom a song. It should

be a song—made of
particulars, wasps,
a gentian—something
immediate, open

scissors, a lady's
eyes—waking
centrifugal, centripetal

Rumba! Rumba!

No, not the downfall
of the Western World
but the wish for its
        downfall
in an idiot mind—
Dance, Baby, dance!

thence springs the conflict,
that it may crash
        hereafter;
not submit and end in
a burst of laughter—
Cha cha, chacha, cha!

to hide the defect—
the difficultly held
burden, to perfect!
melted in a wish to die.
Dance, Baby, dance
        the Cuban Rumba!

A Plea for Mercy

Who hasn't been frustrated
with the eternal virgin
shining before him and he
cold as a stone?

Figueras Castle

Nine truckloads of jewels
while the people starved
Nine truckloads
in the mud

And the people's enemies
coming fast. Stick 'em
in your pockets
the General said,

They're yours, by God and
check them in for the
people at the Consulate
in Perpignan.

But some of them didn't
bother—like those who had
stolen them first
and were not

arrested for it as these were
in their need, not held
for it as these were
in their dire need.

Eternity

She had come, like the river
from up country and had work now
in town—

When? Tonight. The street was
dark, she late. Two
young rips

had cavorted down the hill in
the silence, jabbering. Then
he heard

the click of her heels—at his
age! and the darkness
grew milky

away above him and seemed to
move, coming down. She
appeared

bare headed, in pearl earrings
and a cloak. Where shall
we go?

The boy friend was expecting me
it was hard to
get away.

Where are you supposed to be?
Night, greater than
the cataract

surged in the cisterns of Noah's
chest, enormous night
that makes

of light a fruit, everywhere
active in the dark.
Olympia

would be expecting him, he swam
from her zig-zag through
the dark—

half things bulging and rotted
out, hanging, standing at
false angles,

abandoned! drove thence close
to two hundred miles
filling

the tank once near midnight, To
the left, at the second
car tracks,

brother. And the stars performed
their stated miracles.
The wind

rose and howled toward 3 A.M.
with a dash of rain turning
warm. Swift

or slow from capsule to capsule
of the light he saw between
the stars

the sky! velvet, like a leaf,
in detail and counting at
random there,

continued, later halting under a
street lamp to make
some notes.

Olympia, her face drawn but relieved
said nothing. Breakfast
at seven.

The Hard Listener

The powerless emperor
makes himself dull
writing poems in a garden
while his armies
kill and burn. But we,
in poverty lacking love,
keep some relation
to the truth of man's
infelicity: say
the late flowers, unspoiled
by insects and waiting
only for the cold.

The Controversy

What do you know about it? the Architect said.
The Executive asked me, What the hell
do you know about business?

Is it so arcane? I can read, I said. Isn't it
just to put 4 and take away 5? From whom?
Isn't that all there is to

it? Whom can you best belabor? And do I have
to read the whole *Apologia*
to make up my mind touching

Newman's undecorated place in the world?
    Who?
they both said,—the situation
and its effects? It's because

of unrelated statements such as that that I
have come to have no respect for
what you say, one of them

looked at me and said. The Jews. Oh the
Jews, the Jews! Is Stinkeroo
Mormun a Jew? If not

then the world is safe (from the Jews!) I can
still read and collate experiences
you never dreamed, I

answered them. Nuts! they said. Very well. Nuts!
and decorated nuts and nuts again,
I said, to you, gentlemen.

Perfection

O lovely apple!
beautifully and completely
rotten,
hardly a contour marred—

perhaps a little
shrivelled at the top but that
aside perfect
in every detail! O lovely

apple! what a
deep and suffusing brown
mantles that
unspoiled surface! No one

has moved you
since I placed you on the porch
rail a month ago
to ripen.

No one. No one!

These Purists

Lovely! all the essential parts,
like an oyster without a shell
fresh and sweet tasting, to be
swallowed, chewed and swallowed.

Or better, a brain without a
skull. I remember once a guy in
our anatomy class dropped one
from the third floor window on
an organ grinder in Pine street.

Fertile

You are a typical American woman
you think men grow on trees—

You want love, only love! rarest
of male fruit! Break it open and

in the white of the crisp flesh
find the symmetrical brown seeds.

A Vision of Labor: 1931

In my head the juxtapositions
impossible otherwise to accomplish:
two young rubber-booted ditchdiggers
beside the bed of the dying bishop—
cracking obscene jokes
at the expense of the flabby woman in
the white bathing suit, the weak breaths
of the old man masquerading under
the double suck of the mule-pump

—by the edge of the sea! the shore
exploded away, constructively,
the sewer going down six feet inside
the seawall along the front of
the cottages—not through them
unfortunately—a *cloaca maxima* like
the one under the Roman Forum
which alone made that possible in
that place . . .

        That's it! There, there!
That's the answer. The thing to be
done: Alone made that
possible (before the rest stands)
there in that place.

        The girl lying there
supine in the old rowboat reading an
adventure magazine and the two guys
—six foot three each of them
if they were an inch—washing their
hip-boots off in the stream jerking
from the pump at the finished manhole,

washing their hands, their heads
and faces, cupping their hands to drink
the stuff. Geezus! What the hell
kind of water is that to drink? But
they probably know what they're doing
—and looking down the bank at her
lying flat out there in the heat with
her five-and-ten dark glasses on
to protect her eyes from the sun's
glare—looking down and smiling over
her like insane men.

        When you've been broke
and damned near starving for
five years you get to look that way,
said my cousin who had had a taste
of it. You can't help it. That's
poverty. Both your mind and your body
are affected. But they're just mechanics
damn good ones most of them, like
anybody else.

        —the white suit
pulled up tight into her crotch the
way she was lying there facing them
—till they called it off, threw
the switch and the pump
stopped and the bishop died
and—they turned their backs on it,
flung their boots over their shoulders
and went home.

The Last Turn

Then see it! in distressing
detail—from behind a red light
at 53d and 8th
of a November evening, the jazz
of the cross lights echoing the
crazy weave of the breaking mind:
splash of a half purple, half
naked woman's body whose jeweled
guts the cars drag up and down—
No house but has its brains
blown off by the dark!
Nothing recognizable, the whole one
jittering direction made of all
directions spelling the inexplicable:
pigment upon flesh and flesh
the pigment the genius of a world,
against which rages the fury of
our concepts, artless but supreme.

The End of the Parade

The sentence undulates
raising no song—
It is too old, the
words of it are falling
apart. Only percussion
strokes continue
with weakening
emphasis what was once
cadenced melody
full of sweet breath.

The A, B & C of It

a. Love's very fleas are mine. Enter
   me, worms and all till I crumble
   and steam with it, pullulate
   to be sucked into an orchid.

b. But the fleas were too shy
   didn't want to offend
   recoiled from the odors
   and couldn't unbend.

c. Take me then, Spirit of Loneliness
   insatiable Spirit of Love
   and let be—for Time without
   odor is Time without me.

The Thoughtful Lover

Deny yourself all
half things. Have it
or leave it.

But it will keep—or
it is not worth
the having.

Never start
anything you can't
finish—

However do not lose
faith because you
are starved!

She loves you
she says. Believe it
—tomorrow.

But today
the particulars
of poetry

that difficult art
require
your whole attention.

The Aftermath

The Winnah! pure as snow
courageous as the wind
strong as a tree
deceptive as the moon

All that is the country
fitted into you
for you were born there.
Now it is rewarding you

for the unswerving mind
curious as a fox
which fox-like escaped
breathless to its hole.

They say you have grown
thinner and that
there is a girl now to
add to the blue eyed boy.

Good! the air of the
uplands is stimulating.

The Storm

A perfect rainbow! a wide
arc low in the northern sky
spans the black lake

troubled by little waves
over which the sun
south of the city shines in

coldly from the bare hill
supine to the wind which
cannot waken anything

but drives the smoke from
a few lean chimneys streaming
violently southward

The Forgotten City

When with my mother I was coming down
from the country the day of the hurricane,
trees were across the road and small branches
kept rattling on the roof of the car
There was ten feet or more of water
making the parkways impassible with wind
bringing more rain in sheets. Brown torrents
gushed up through new sluices in the
valley floor so that I had to take what road
I could find bearing to the south and west,
to get back to the city. I passed through
extraordinary places, as vivid as any
I ever saw where the storm had broken
the barrier and let through
a strange commonplace: Long, deserted avenues
with unrecognized names at the corners and
drunken looking people with completely
foreign manners. Monuments, institutions
and in one place a large body of water
startled me with an acre or more of hot
jets spouting up symmetrically over it. Parks.
I had no idea where I was and promised myself
I would some day go back to study this
curious and industrious people who lived
in these apartments, at these sharp
corners and turns of intersecting avenues
with so little apparent communication
with an outside world. How did they get
cut off this way from representation in our
newspapers and other means of publicity
when so near the metropolis, so closely
surrounded by the familiar and the famous?

The Yellow Chimney

There is a plume
of fleshpale
smoke upon the blue

sky. The silver
rings that
strap the yellow

brick stack at
wide intervals shine
in this amber

light—not
of the sun not of
the pale sun but

his born brother
the
declining season

The Bare Tree

The bare cherry tree
higher than the roof
last year produced
abundant fruit. But how
speak of fruit confronted
by that skeleton?
Though live it may be
there is no fruit on it.
Therefore chop it down
and use the wood
against this biting cold.

Raleigh Was Right

We cannot go to the country
for the country will bring us
    no peace
What can the small violets tell us
that grow on furry stems in
the long grass among lance shaped
    leaves?

Though you praise us
and call to mind the poets
who sung of our loveliness
it was long ago!
long ago! when country people
would plow and sow with
flowering minds and pockets
    at ease—
if ever this were true.

Not now. Love itself a flower
with roots in a parched ground.
Empty pockets make empty heads.
Cure it if you can but
do not believe that we can live
today in the country
for the country will bring us
    no peace.

The Monstrous Marriage

She who with innocent and tender hands
reached up to take the wounded
pigeon from the branch, found it turn

into a fury as it bled. Maddened she clung
to it stabbed by its pain and the blood
of her hands and the bird's blood

mingled while she stilled it for the moment
and wrapped it in her thought's
clean white handkerchief. After that

she adopted a hawk's life as her own.
For it looked up and said, You are
my wife for this. Then she released him.

But he came back shortly. Certainly,
since we are married, she said to him, no
one will accept it. Time passed.

I try to imitate you, he said while she
cried a little in smiling. Mostly,
he confided, my head is clouded

except for hunting. But for parts of
a day it's clear as any man's—by
your love. No, she would

answer him pitifully, what clearer than
a hawk's eye and reasonably the
mind also must be so. He turned his

head and seeing his profile in her
mirror ruffled his feathers and gave
a hawk's cry, desolately.

Nestling upon her as was his wont he
hid his talons from her soft flesh
fluttering his wings against her sides

until her mind, always astonished at
his assumptions, agonized, heard
footsteps and hurried him to

the open window whence he made off.
After that she had a leather belt made
upon which he perched to enjoy her.

Sometimes *It Turns Dry and the Leaves Fall before They Are Beautiful*

This crystal sphere
upon whose edge I drive
turns brilliantly—
The level river shines!

My love! My love!
how sadly do we thrive:
thistle-caps and
sumac or a tree whose

sharpened leaves
perfect as they are
look no farther than—
into the grass.

Sparrows Among Dry Leaves

The sparrows by the iron fence post—
hardly seen for the dry leaves
that half cover them—
stirring up the leaves, fight
and chirp stridently, search and
peck the sharp gravel to
good digestion and love's
obscure and insatiable appetite.

Prelude to Winter

The moth under the eaves
with wings like
the bark of a tree, lies
symmetrically still—

And love is a curious
soft-winged thing
unmoving under the eaves
when the leaves fall.

Silence

Under a low sky—
this quiet morning
of red and
yellow leaves—

a bird disturbs
no more than one twig
of the green leaved
peach tree

Another Year

In the rose garden in the park
let us learn how little there is
          to fear
from the competition of conflicting
          seasons—
and avoid comparisons,
alone in that still place.
The slender quietness of the old
          bushes
is of a virtue all its own . . .

A Cold Front

This woman with a dead face
has seven foster children
and a new baby of her own in
spite of that. She wants pills

for an abortion and says,
Uh hum, in reply to me while
her blanketed infant makes
unrelated grunts of salutation.

She looks at me with her mouth
open and blinks her expressionless
carved eyes, like a cat
on a limb too tired to go higher

from its tormentors. And still
the baby chortles in its spit
and there is a dull flush
almost of beauty to the woman's face

as she says, looking at me
quietly, I won't have any more.
In a case like this I know
quick action is the main thing.

Against the Sky

Let me not forget at least,
after the three day rain,
beaks raised aface, the two starlings
at and near the top twig

of the white-oak, dwarfing
the barn, completing the minute
green of the sculptured foliage, their
bullet heads bent back, their horny

lips chattering to the morning
sun! Praise! while the
wraithlike warblers, all but unseen
in looping flight dart from

pine to spruce, spruce to pine
southward. Southward! where
new mating warms the wit and cold
does not strike, for respite.

An Address

Walk softly on my grave
for I desired you,

a matter for sorrow
for decay;

flowers without odor
garlanded

about the sad legend:
Live in this

whom green youth denied.

The Gentle Rejoinder

These are the days I want to
give up my job and join
the old men I once saw
on the wharf at Villefranche
fishing for sea-snails,
with a split stick,
in the shallow water—

              I know
something else you could catch,
she said, in the spring
as easily, if you
wanted to. But you probably
don't want to, do you?

To Ford Madox Ford in Heaven

Is it any better in Heaven, my friend Ford,
    than you found it in Provence?

I don't think so for you made Provence a
    heaven by your praise of it
to give a foretaste of what might be
    your joy in the present circumstances.
It was Heaven you were describing there
    transubstantiated from its narrowness
to resemble the paths and gardens of a
    greater world where you now reside.
But, dear man, you have taken a major
    part of it from us.
        Provence that you
praised so well will never be the same
    Provence to us
        now you are gone.

A heavenly man you seem to me now, never
    having been for me a saintly one.
It lived about you, a certain grossness that
    was not like the world.
The world is cleanly, polished and well
    made but heavenly man
is filthy with his flesh and corrupt that
    loves to eat and drink and whore—
to laugh at himself and not be afraid of
    himself knowing well he has
no possessions and opinions that are worth
    caring a broker's word about
and that all he is, but one thing, he feeds
    as one will feed a pet dog.

So roust and love and dredge the belly full
    in Heaven's name!
I laugh to think of you wheezing in Heaven.
    Where is Heaven? But why
do I ask that, since you showed the way?
    I don't care a damn for it
other than for that better part lives beside
    me here so long as I
live and remember you. Thank God you
    were not delicate, you let the world in
and lied! damn it you lied grossly
    sometimes. But it was all, I
see now, a carelessness, the part of a man
    that is homeless here on earth.

Provence, the fat assed Ford will never
    again strain the chairs of your cafés
pull and pare for his dish your sacred garlic,
    grunt and sweat and lick
his lips. Gross as the world he has left to
    us he has become
a part of that of which you were the known
    part, Provence, he loved so well.

The Clouds

Aigeltinger

In the bare trees old husks make new designs
Love moves the crows before the dawn
The cherry-sun ushers in the new phase

The radiant mind
addressed by tufts of flocking pear blossoms
proposes new profundities to the soul

Deftness stirs in the cells
of Aigeltinger's brain which flares
like ribbons round an electric fan

This is impressive, he will soon proclaim
God!

And round and round, the winds
and underfoot, the grass
the rose-cane leaves and blackberries
and Jim will read the encyclopedia to his
new bride—gradually

Aigeltinger you have stuck in my conk
illuminating, for nearly half a century I
could never beat you at your specialty

Nothing has ever beaten a mathematician
but yeast

The cloudless sky takes the sun in its periphery
and slides its disc across the blue

They say I'm not profound

But where is profundity, Aigeltinger
mathematical genius
dragged drunk from some cheap bar to serve
their petty purposes?

Aigeltinger, you were profound

Franklin Square

Instead of
the flower of the hawthorn
the spine:

The tree is in bloom
the flowers
and the leaves together

sheltering
the noisy sparrows
that give

by their intimate
indifference,
the squirrels and pigeons

on the sharp-
edged lawns—the figure
of a park:

A city, a decadence
of bounty—
a tall negress approaching

the bench
pursing her old mouth
for what coin?

Labrador

How clean these shallows
how firm these rocks stand
about which wash
the waters of the world

It is ice to this body
that unclothes its pallors
to thoughts
of an immeasurable sea,

unmarred, that as it lifts
encloses this
straining mind, these
limbs in a single gesture.

The Apparition

My greetings to you, sir, whose memory,
the striped coat and colors— What is one man?
a man remembered still in the jacket
of his success? of the winning club?
in himself—successful? one man, alone?
This is that he who slights his fellows—
or else, as he is, plunges
to the wind-whipped swirl, hat, coat, shoes
and—as you did—drags in the body
to the grapples defying death and the sea.
Not once but—again!
Is this the war—that spawned you? Or
did you make the war? Whichever, there you are.

The Light Shall Not Enter

It is in the minds
of the righteous
that death crows loudest.

Death! the cry is. Death!
in the teeth
of the sky, as though

fire is not to blast
and the copper of desire
burnish under it. Oh

we choose our words
too carefully
to fit a calcined skeleton

of meaning, in which
lives! lives only resent-
ment. We the flame

and furnace talk, embittered
as though ours were
some other

destiny whose entrails
are not to burn—shall
escape the heat. Pah!

A Woman in Front of a Bank

The bank is a matter of columns,
like . convention,
unlike invention; but the pediments
sit there in the sun

to convince the doubting of
investments "solid
as rock"—upon which the world
stands, the world of finance,

the only world: Just there,
talking with another woman while
rocking a baby carriage
back and forth stands a woman in

a pink cotton dress, bare legged
and headed whose legs
are two columns to hold up
her face, like Lenin's (her loosely

arranged hair profusely blond) or
Darwin's and there you
have it:
a woman in front of a bank.

The Night Rider

Scoured like a conch
or the moon's shell
I ride from my love
through the damp night.

there are lights
through the trees,
falling leaves,
the air and the blood

an even mood
warm with summer dwindling,
relic of heat:
Ruin dearly bought

smoothed to a round
carved by the sand
the pulse a remembered pulse
of full-tide gone

Chanson

This woman! how shall I describe her
who is wealthly in the riches
of her sex? No counterfeit, no mere
metal to be sure—

yet, a treasury, a sort of lien upon
all property we list and transfer.
This woman has no need to play the market
or to do anything more than watch

the moon. For to her, thoughts are not
like those of the philosopher
or scientist, or clever playwright.
Her thoughts are to her

like fruit to the tree, the apple, pear.
She thinks and thinks well, but
to different purpose than a man, and I
discover there a novel territory.

It is a world to make the world
little worth travelling by ship or air.
Moscow, Zanzibar, the Ægean
Islands, the Crimea she surpasses

by that which by her very being she
would infer, a New World
welcome as to a sailor and habitable
so that I am willing to stay there.

The Birdsong

Disturb the balance, broken bird
the distress of the song
cuts through an ample silence
sweeping the trees.

It is the trouble
of the brook that makes it loud,
the current broke to give
out a burbling

breaks the arched stillness,
ripples the tall grass
gone to heady seed, bows the heads ·
of goldenrod

that bear a vulgar happiness,
the bay-berry,
briars—
break also your happiness for me.

To a Lovely Old Bitch

Sappho, Sappho, Sappho! initiate,
handmaiden, to Astarte,
you praised delicate flowers

and likened them
to virgins of your acquaintance.
Let them grow, thank God!
outside the cemetery barrier:

—burials for cash,
the shares ample security
against—?

The butterfly,
The Painted Admiral,
on a milkweed cluster,
untrampled,
keep you company and pale
blue chickory, frilled
petals

—butter-and-eggs,
lady's-slipper, close beside
the rust of the dump-heap
—rust, broken fruit-baskets
and bits of plaster,
painted on one side,

from dismantled bedrooms.

The Bitter World of Spring

On a wet pavement the white sky recedes
mottled black by the inverted
pillars of the red elms,
in perspective, that lift the tangled

net of their desires hard into
the falling rain. And brown smoke
is driven down, running like
water over the roof of the bridge-

keeper's cubicle. And, as usual,
the fight as to the nature of poetry
—Shall the philosophers capture it?—
is on. And, casting an eye

down into the water, there, announced
by the silence of a white
bush in flower, close
under the bridge, the shad ascend,

midway between the surface and the mud,
and you can see their bodies
red-finned in the dark
water headed, unrelenting, upstream.

Lament

What face, in the water,
distinct
yet washed by an obscurity?

The willow supplants its own
struggling rafters
(of winter branches)

by a green radiance. Is it
old or young?
But what this face

reflected beyond the bare structures
of a face
shining from the creaseless

water? A face
overlaid with evil, brown water;
the good insecure, the evil

sure beyond the buried sun. Lift
it. Turn away.
There was beside you

but now another face,
with long nose and clear blue eyes,
secure . . .

A History of Love

1

And would you gather turds
for your grandmother's garden?
Out with you then, dustpan and broom;
she has seen the horse passing!

Out you go, bold again
as you promise always to be.
Stick your tongue out at the neighbors
that her flowers may grow.

Let me stress your
          loveliness
and its gravity

its counter-hell: Reading
finds you on the page

where sight enlarges
to confound the mind
          and only

a child is frightened
by its father's headgear

while a bird jigs and ol' Bunk
Johnson blows his horn.

3

With the mind and with the hand,
by moral turn and prestidigitation
fan the smouldering flame of love
which in the dull coals is all but gone.

Between one and the other transpose
wrong and rouse
the banished smile that used to spring
at once at meeting!

Rewaken love, again, again! to warm
the chilly heart and bring fresh flowers.
For flowers are not, as we are not
of that stuff whence we both are got.

When Structure Fails
Rhyme Attempts to Come to the Rescue

The old horse dies slow.
By gradual degrees
the fervor of his veins
matches the leaves'

stretch, day by day. But
the pace that his
mind keeps is the pace
of his dreams. He

does what he can, with
unabated phlegm,
ahem! but the pace that
his flesh keeps—

leaning, leaning upon
the bars—beggars
by far all pace and every
refuge of his dreams.

Education a Failure

The minor stupidities
of my world
dominate that world—
as when

with two bridges across
the river and one
closed for repairs
the other also

will be closed by
the authorities
for painting! But then
there is heaven

and the ideal state
closed also
before the aspiring soul.
I had rather

watch a cat threading
a hedge with
another sitting by
while the bird

screams overhead
athrash
in the cover of the
low branches.

The Banner Bearer

In the rain, the lonesome
dog idiosyn-
cratically, with each
quadribeat, throws

out the left fore-
foot beyond
the right intent, in
his stride,

on some obscure
insistence—from bridge-
ward going
into new territory.

The Goat

Having in the mind thought
to have died,
to that celebrant
among trees, aging (with the season)
foreign to sight—

in a field a goat, befouled,
shagbellied, indifferent to
the mind's ecstasies,
flutters its blunt tail

and turns a vacant face
lop-eared, sleepy-eyed to stare,
unblinking, meditant—
listless
in its assured sanctity.

Two Deliberate Exercises

(*for Agnes*)

In a fourfold silence the music
struggles for mastery and the mind
from its silence, fatefully assured,
wakens to the music: Unnamed,
without age, sex or pretence of
accomplishment—their faces
blank, they rise and move
to the platform unannounced and
the music leads them—the racially
stigmaed, the gross bodied, all
feet—cleansing from each
his awkwardness for him to blossom
thence a sound pleading,
pleading for pleasure, pleasure!
at the tunnel of the ear. And love,
who hides from public places,
moves in his bed of air, of flowers,
of ducks, of sheep and locust
trees in bloom—the white, sweet
locust—to fade again
at the sounds into
impossibilities and thunderstorms.
        There remains the good teacher
blinking from his dream before
the hand-shakes of his constituents.

In the center, above the basin,
the mirror. To the left of
it the Maxfield Parrish, Ulysses
at Sea, his small ship coming
fog-threatened from between
Scylla and Charybdis. And
to the right the girl of nine,
play-pail in hand, bareheaded upon
a dune-crest facing the shining
waters. There you have it,
unexcelled as feeling. What
of it? Well, we live among
the birds and bees in vain unless
there result—now or then—
a presentation to which
these two presentations serve
as humble stopgaps—to invoke
for us a whole realm, compact of
inverted nature, straining
within the imprisoned mind to
free us. Well, to free us.

       At which, seeing in the pasture
horses among the brambles,
hearing the wind sigh,
we broach the chaos—unless
Valéry be mistaken—of
the technical where stand waiting
for us or nowhere the tree-
lined avenues of our desires.

The Mirrors

Is Germany's bestiality, in detail
like certain racial traits,
any more than a reflection of the world's

evil? Take a negative, take Ezra Pound
for example, and see
how the world has impressed itself

there. It is as when with infra-red
searching a landscape obscured
to the unaided eye one discloses

the sea. The world is at its worst the
positive to these foils,
imaged there as on the eyes of a fly.

His Daughter

Her jaw wagging
her left hand pointing
stiff armed
behind her, I noticed:

her youth, her
receding chin and
fair hair;
her legs, bare

The sun was on her
as she came
to the step's edge,
the fat man,

caught in his stride,
collarless,
turned sweating
toward her.

Design for November

Let confusion be the design
and all my thoughts go,
swallowed by desire: recess
from promises in
the November of your arms.
Release from the rose: broken
reeds, strawpale,
through which, from easy
branches that mock the blood
a few leaves fall. There
the mind is cradled,
stripped also and returned
to the ground, a trivial
and momentary clatter. Sleep
and be brought down and so
condone the world, eased of
the jagged sky and all
its petty imageries, flying
birds, its fogs and windy
phalanxes . . .

The Manoeuvre

I saw the two starlings
coming in toward the wires.
But at the last,
just before alighting, they

turned in the air together
and landed backwards!
that's what got me—to
face into the wind's teeth.

The Horse

The horse moves
independently
without reference
to his load

He has eyes
like a woman and
turns them
about, throws

back his ears
and is generally
conscious of
the world. Yet

he pulls when
he must and
pulls well, blowing
fog from

his nostrils
like fumes from
the twin
exhausts of a car.

Hard Times

Stone steps, a solid
block too tough
to be pried out, from
which the house,

rather, has been
avulsed leaving
a pedestal, on which
a fat boy in

an old overcoat, a
butt between
his thick lips, the
coat pushed back,

stands kidding,
Parking Space! three
steps up from his
less lucky fellows.

The Dish of Fruit

The table describes
nothing: four legs, by which
it becomes a table. Four lines
by which it becomes a quatrain,

the poem that lifts the dish
of fruit, if we say it is like
a table—how will it describe
the contents of the poem?

The Motor-Barge

The motor-barge is
at the bridge the
air lead
the broken ice

unmoving. A gull,
the eternal
gull, flies as
always, eyes alert

beak pointing
to the life-giving
water. Time
falters but for

the broad river-
craft which
low in the water
moves grad-

ually, edging
between the smeared
bulkheads,
churning a mild

wake, laboring
to push past
the constriction
with its heavy load

Russia

The Williams Avenue Zionist Church
                              (colored)
a thing to hold in the palm of the hand,
your big hand—
the dwarf campanile piled up, improvised
of blue cinder-blocks, badly aligned
(except for the incentive)

                              unvarnished,
the cross at the top slapped together
(in this lumber shortage) of sticks from
an old barrel top, I think

                    —painted white

Russia, idiot of the world, blind idiot
—do you understand me?

                              This also
I place in your hands . . .

I dream! and my dream is folly. While
armies rush to the encounter
I, alone, dream before the impending
onslaught. And the power in me,
to be crushed out: this paper, forgotten
—not even known ever to have existed,
proclaims the power of my dream . . .

Folly! I call upon folly to save us—
and scandal and disapproval, the restless
angels of the mind—

                              (I omit
the silly word exile. For from what and
to what land shall I be exiled and talk of
the cardinal bird and the starling
as though they were strange?)

                              I am
at home in my dream, Russia; and only there,
before the obliterating blow
                    that shall flatten everything
and its crazy masonry,
                    am I at home.

Inspired by my dream I do not call upon
a party to save me, nor a government
of whatever sort.

                    Rather I descend into
my dream as into a quiet lake
and there, already there, I find
my kinships, Thence I rise by my own
propulsions into a world beyond the moon.

O Russia, Russia! must we begin to call
you idiot of the world? When
you were a dream the world lived in you
inviolate—

O Russia! Russians! come with me into
my dream and let us be lovers,
connoisseurs, idlers—Come with me
in the sprit of Walt Whitman's earliest
poem, let us loaf at our ease—a moment
at the edge of destruction

                    Look.
Look through my eyes a moment. I am
a poet, uninfluential, with no skill
in polemics—my friends tell me I lack
the intellect. Look,
I once met Mayakovsky. Remember
Mayakovsky? I have a little paper-bound
volume of his in my attic, inscribed by him
in his scrawling hand to our mutual
friendship. He put one foot up
on the table that night at 14th St. when
he read to us—and his voice came
like the outpourings of the Odyssey.

                    Russians!
let Mayakovsky be my sponsor—he
and his Willie, the Havana street-cleaner—
Mayakovsky was a good guy and killed
himself, I suppose, not to embarrass you.

And so I go about.

And now I want to call your attention—
that you may know what keen eyes
I have in my dream—
to Leonardo's Last Supper! a small print
I saw today in a poor kitchen.

                    Russia!
for the first time in my life, I noticed
this famous picture not because
of the subject matter but because
of the severity and simplicity
of the background! Oh there was
the passion of the scene, of course,
generally. But particularly,

ignoring the subject, I fell upon
the perpendiculars of the paneled
woodwork standing there, submissive,
in exaggerated perspective.

There you have it. It's that background
from which my dreams have sprung. These
I dedicate now to you, now when I am
about to die. I hold back nothing. I lay
my spirit at your feet and say to you:
Here I am, a dreamer. I do not
resist you. Among many others, undistinguished,
of no moment—I am the background
upon which you will build your empire.

The Act

There were the roses, in the rain.
Don't cut them, I pleaded.
            They won't last, she said
But they're so beautiful
            where they are.
Agh, we were all beautiful once, she
            said,
and cut them and gave them to me
            in my hand.

The Savage Beast

As I leaned to retrieve
my property
he leaped with all his weight
so that I felt

the wind of his jaws
as his teeth gnashed
before my mouth.
Isn't he awful! said

the woman, his collar
straining under her clutch.
Yes, I replied drily
wanting to eviscerate

the thing there, scoop
out his brains
and eat them—and hers
too! Until it flashed

on me, How many, like
this dog, could I not wish
had been here in my
place, only a little closer!

The Well Disciplined Bargeman

The shadow does not move. It is the water moves,
running out. A monolith of sand on a passing barge,
riding the swift water, makes that its fellow.

Standing upon the load the well disciplined bargeman
rakes it carefully, smooth on top with nicely squared
edges to conform to the barge outlines—ritually: sand.

All about him the silver water, fish-swift, races
under the Presence. Whatever there is else is moving.
The restless gulls, unlike companionable pigeons,

taking their cue from the ruffled water, dip and circle
avidly into the gale. Only the bargeman raking
upon his barge remains, like the shadow, sleeping

Raindrops on a Briar

I, a writer, at one time hipped on
painting, did not consider
the effects, painting,
for that reason, static, on

the contrary the stillness of
the objects—the flowers, the gloves—
freed them precisely by that
from a necessity merely to move

in space as if they had been—
not children! but the thinking male
or the charged and deliver-
ing female frantic with ecstasies;

served rather to present, for me,
a more pregnant motion: a
series of varying leaves
clinging still, let us say, to

the cat-briar after last night's
storm, its waterdrops
ranged upon the arching stems
irregularly as an accompaniment.

Suzanne

Brother Paul! look!
—but he rushes to a different
window.
The moon!

I heard shrieks and thought:
What's that?

That's just Suzanne
talking to the moon!
Pounding on the window
with both fists:

    Paul!   Paul!

—and talking to the moon.
Shrieking
and pounding the glass
with both fists!

Brother Paul! the moon!

Navajo

Red woman,
    (Keep Christ out
    of this—and
    his mountains:
    Sangre de Cristo
    red rocks that make
    the water run
    blood-red)
squaw in red
red woman
walking the desert
I suspected
I should remember
you this way:
    walking the brain
    eyes cast down
    to escape ME!
    with fixed sight
    stalking
    the grey brush
    paralleling
    the highway . . .
    —head mobbled
    red, red
    to the ground—
    sweeping the
    ground—
    the blood walking
    erect, the
    desert animating
    the blood to walk
    erect by choice
    through

                    the pale green
                    of the starveling
                    sage

Graph

                    There was another, too
                    a half-breed Cherokee
                    tried to thumb a ride
                    out of Tulsa, standing there
                    with a bunch of wildflowers
                    in her left hand
                    pressed close
                    just below the belly

The Testament of Perpetual Change

Mortal Prudence, handmaid of divine Providence
    Walgreen carries Culture to the West:
hath inscrutable reckoning with Fate and Fortune:
    At Cortez, Colorado the Indian prices
We sail a changeful sea through halcyon days and storm,
    a bottle of cheap perfume, furtively—
and when the ship laboreth, our stedfast purpose
    but doesn't buy, while under my hotel window
trembles like as a compass in a binnacle.
    a Radiance Rose spreads its shell—thin
Our stability is but balance, and wisdom lies
    petals above the non-irrigated garden
in masterful administration of the unforeseen
    among the unprotected desert foliage.

'Twas late in my long journey when I had clomb to where
    Having returned from Mesa Verde, the ruins
the path was narrowing and the company few
    of the Cliff Dwellers' palaces still in possession
                  of my mind

The Flower

This too I love
Flossie sitting in the sun
on its cane
the first rose

yellow as an egg the pet
canary
in his cage
beside her carolling

For a Low Voice

If you ignore the possibilities of art,
huh, huh, huh, huh, huh, &c.
you are likely to become involved,
huh! in extreme, huh, huh, huh, huh, huh

&c. difficulties. For instance, when
they started to make a park
at the site of the old Dutch, huh, huh, huh!
cemetery, ha, ha, ha, ha, ha, &c.

they could not, digging down
upon the hoary, heh, heh! graves,
find so much as a thighbone, huh, huh, huh!
or in fact anything! wha, ha,

ha, ha, ha, ha, ha, ha, &c.
to remove! This,
according to the requirements of the case,
created a huh, huh, huh, huh

shall we say, dilemma? So that,
to make a gesture, for old time's sake,
heh, heh! of filling
the one vault retained as communal repository

huh, huh! and monument, they
had to throw in SOMETHING! presumed
to be bones but observed by those nearest,
heh, heh, heh! more to resemble

rotten tree roots than ossa!
a low sort of dissembling, ha, ha, ha, &c.
on the part of the officials
were it not excusable, oh, ho, ho, ho, ho, &c.

under the head of . . . Yes, yes, of course!
wha, ha, ha, ha, ha, ha! Whoh, ho,
hee, hee! Rather a triumph of
a sort! Whoop la! Whee hee!—don't you think?

The Words Lying Idle

The fields parched, the leaves
drying on the maples, the birds' beaks
gaping! if it would rain,
if it would only rain! Clouds come up,
move from the west and from the south
but they bring no rain. Heat and dry winds
—the grass is curled and brittle underfoot,
the foot leaves it broken. The roads are dust.

But the mind is dust also
and the eyes burn from it. They burn more
from restless nights, from the full moon shining
on a dry earth than from lack of rain.
The rain, if it fell, would ease the mind
more than the grass, the mind would
be somewhat, at least, appeased against
this dryness and the death implied.

Picture of a Nude in a Machine Shop

and foundry,
               (that's art)
        a red ostrich plume
in her hair:

Sweat and muddy water,
coiled fuse-strips
               surround her
poised sitting—
(between red, parted
               curtains)

the right leg
               (stockinged)
up!
        beside the point—
at ease.

Light as a glove, light
as her black gloves!
Modeled as a shoe, a woman's
high heeled shoe!

—the other leg stretched
out
        bare
               (toward the top—
and upward)
               as
the smeared hide under
shirt and pants
stiff with grease and dirt
is bare—

                        approaching
        the centrum

                        (disguised)
        the metal to be devalued!

                        —bare as
        a blow-torch flame,
                        undisguised.

The Hurricane

                The tree lay down
                on the garage roof
                and stretched, You
                have your heaven,
                it said, go to it.

The Mind's Games

If a man can say of his life or
any moment of his life, There is
nothing more to be desired! his state
becomes like that told in the famous
double sonnet—but without the
sonnet's restrictions. Let him go look
at the river flowing or the bank
of late flowers, there will be one
small fly still among the petals
in whose gauzy wings raised above
its back a rainbow shines. The world
to him is radiant and even the fact
of poverty is wholly without despair.

So it seems until there rouse
to him pictures of the systematically
starved—for a purpose, at the mind's
proposal. What good then the
light winged fly, the flower or
the river—too foul to drink of or
even to bathe in? The 90 storey building
beyond the ocean that a rocket
will span for destruction in a matter
of minutes but will not
bring him, in a century, food or
relief of any sort from his suffering.

The world too much with us? Rot!
the world is not half enough with us—
the rot of a potato with
a healthy skin, a rot that is
never revealed till we are about to
eat—and it revolts us. Beauty?

Beauty should make us paupers,
should blind us, rob us—for it
does not feed the sufferer but makes
his suffering a fly-blown putrescence
and ourselves decay—unless
the ecstasy be general.

The Stylist

Long time no see.
     —a flash as
from polished steel,
then:

I've been too
damned poor to get out
of the woods. I was
expecting you
to come up and bring
me into town.

No answer.

Note to Music:
Brahms 1st Piano Concerto

Of music, in a cavernous house,
we enjoy our humanity the more
being by machine, since it is lost,
survives, is rekindled only
ad interim, pending a willed
refusal: the Demuths, the Sheelers,
the Hartleys, green and grey;
black (the meaning crimson)
are moved likewise in us thereby.

We falter to assurance in despair
hearing the piano pant to
the horns' uncertain blow that
octaves sidelong from the deafened
windows crescendo, rallentando,
diminuendo in wave-like dogmas
we no longer will. Let us sob
and sonnet our dreams, breathing
upon our nails before the savage
snow . . .

The Red-Wing Blackbird

The wild red-wing black
bird croaks frog
like though more shrill
as the beads of

his eyes blaze over the
swamp and the o-
dors of the swamp vodka
to his nostrils

A Place (Any Place) to Transcend All Places

In New York, it is said,
they do meet (if that is
what is wanted) talk but
nothing is exchanged
unless that guff
can be retranslated: as
to say, that is not
the end, there are channels
above that, draining
places from which New York
is dignified, created (the
deaf are not tuned in).

A church in New Hampshire
built by its pastor
from his own wood lot. One
black (of course, red)
rose; a fat old woman backing
through a screen door. Two,
from the armpits
down, contrasting in bed,
breathless; a letter from
a ship; leaves filling,
making, a tree (but
wait) not just leaves,
leaves of one design that
make a certain design,
no two alike, not like
the locust either, next in line,
nor the Rose of Sharon, in
the pod-stage, near it—a
tree! Imagine it! Pears
philosophically hard. Nor

thought that is from
branches on a root, from
an acid soil, with scant
grass about the bole
where it breaks through.

New York is built of
such grass and weeds; a
                    modern
tuberculin-tested herd
white-faced behind a
white fence, patient and
uniform; a museum of looks
across a breakfast
table; subways of dreams;
towers of divisions
from thin pay envelopes.
What else is it? And what
else can it be? Sweatshops
and railroad yards at dusk
(puffed up by fantasy
to seem real) what else
can they be budded on
to live a little longer?
The eyes by this
far quicker than the mind.

              —and we have
:Southern writers, foreign
writers, hugging a dis-
tinction, while perspectived
behind them following
the crisis (at home)
peasant loyalties inspire
the avant-garde. Abstractly?
No: That was for something

else. "Le futur!" grimly.
New York? That hodge-
                    podge?
The international city
(from the Bosphorus). Poor
Hoboken. Poor sad
Eliot. Poor memory.
                    —and we have
: the memory of Elsa
von Freytag Loringhofen,
a fixation from the street
door of a Berlin
playhouse; all who "wear
their manner too obviously,"
the adopted English (white)
and many others.

                    —and we have
: the script writer advising
"every line to be like
a ten word telegram" but
neglecting to add, "to a
child of twelve"—obscene
beyond belief.

                    Obscene and
abstract as excrement—
that no one wants to own
except the coolie
with a garden of which
the lettuce particularly
depends on it—if you
like lettuce, but
very, very specially, heaped
about the roots for nourish-
                    ment.

The Old House

Rescued! new-white

               (from Time's
dragon: neglect-tastelessness—
the down-beat)

          But why?
why the descent into ugliness that
intervened, how
could it have come about,
               (the essence—
cluttered with weeds, broken gear
—in a shoddy neighborhood)
              something so sound?

—that there should have befallen
such decay, such decay of the senses—
the redundant and expensive,
the useless, the useless rhyme?

Stasis:
        a balance of . . .
vacuities, seeking . . . to
achieve . . . by emphasis!
the full sonorities of . . . an
evasion! !

        —lack of
"virtue," the fake castellation, the
sham tower—upon a hidden
weakness of trusses, a whole period
shot to hell out of disrelatedness
to mind, to object association:

the years following
the Civil War—

But four
balanced gables, in a good old style,
four symmetrical waves,
                    well anchored,
turning about the roof's pivot,
simple and direct,
                    how could they not
have apprehended it? They could not—
Bitter reminder.

And then!
out of the air, out of decay, out of
desire, necessity, through
economic press—aftermath of "the bomb"—
a Perseus! rescue comes:

                    —the luminous
from "sea wrack," sets it, for itself,
a house almost gone, shining again.

The Thing

Each time it rings
I think it is for
me but it is
not for me nor for

anyone it merely
rings and we
serve it bitterly
together, they and I

The Mind Hesitant

Sometimes the river
becomes a river in the mind
or of the mind
or in and of the mind

Its banks snow
the tide falling a dark
rim lies between
the water and the shore

And the mind hesitant
regarding the stream
senses
a likeness which it

will find—a complex
image: something
of white brows
bound by a ribbon

of sooty thought
beyond, yes well beyond
the mobile features
of swiftly

flowing waters, before
the tide will
change
and rise again, maybe

Tragic Detail

The day before I died
I noticed the maple tree
how its bark curled
against the November blaze

There was some work
to do and three birds
stepped awkwardly abreast
upon the bare lawn

Only the country-woman's
lip soft with down
black as her hair was black
against the white skin

comforted me but the twins
and their sister
excluded me dragging
insistent upon the loose gown.

Philomena Andronico

With the boys busy
at ball
in the worn lot
nearby

She stands in
the short street
reflectively bouncing
the red ball

Slowly
practiced
a little awkwardly
throwing one leg over

(Not as she had done
formerly
screaming and
missing

But slowly
surely) then
pausing throws
the ball

With a full slow
very slow
and easy motion
following through

With a slow
half turn—
as the ball flies
and rolls gently

At the child's feet
waiting—
and yet he misses
it and turns

And runs while she
slowly
regains her former
pose

Then shoves her fingers
up through
her loose short hair
quickly

Draws one stocking
tight and
waiting
tilts

Her hips and
in the warm still
air lets
her arms
       Fall

Fall
loosely
(waiting)
at her sides

The Woodpecker

Innocence! Innocence is the condition of heaven.
Only in that which we do not yet know shall we
be fêted, fed. That is to say, with ceremony. The
unknown is our refuge toward which we hurtle. For
even tho', lacking parachute, we be flattened
upon the earth it will not be the same earth we left
to fly upward. To seek what? There is nothing
there. It is not even the unknown for us now. But
we never knew the earth so solidly as when we were
crushed upon it. From a height we fall, innocent,
to our deaths.

                  I'd rather in the November
be a woodpecker of the woods. A cry, a movement,
red dabbled, among the bare branches. A light, a
destination where destinations are endless and
the beetle the end of flight. Fed and the ceremony
unwitnessed other than by the lichened rocks, the
dry leaves and the upright bodies of the trees.
It is innocence flings the black and white body
through the air, innocence guides him. Flight
means only desire and desire the end of flight,
stabbing there with a barbed tongue which *succeeds*!

The Girl

with big breasts
under a blue sweater

bareheaded—
crossing the street

reading a newspaper
stops, turns

and looks down
as though

she had seen a dime
on the pavement

The Clouds

I

Filling the mind
upon the rim of the overarching sky, the
      horses of
the dawn charge from south to north,
      gigantic beasts
rearing flame-edged above the pit,
a rank confusion of the imagination still
      uncured
a rule, piebald under the streetlamps,
      reluctant
to be torn from its hold.

                Their flanks still
caught among low, blocking forms their
      fore-parts
rise lucid beyond this smell of a swamp, a mud
livid with decay and life! turtles
that burrowing among the white roots lift
      their green
red-striped faces startled before the dawn.

A black flag, writhing and whipping at the
      staff-head
mounts the sepulcher of the empty bank,
      fights
to be free . . .
        South to north! the direction
unmistakable, they move, distinct beyond
      the unclear
edge of the world, clouds! like statues
before which we are drawn—in darkness,

        thinking of
our dead, unable, knowing no place
where else rightly to lodge them.

                                Tragic outlines
and the bodies of horses, mindfilling—but
visible! against the invisible; actual against
the imagined and the concocted; unspoiled
        by hands
and unshaped also by them but caressed by
        sight only,
moving among them, not that that propels
the eyes from under, while it blinds:

—upon whose backs the dead ride, high!
undirtied by the putridity we fasten upon
        them—
South to north, for this moment distinct
        and undeformed,
into the no-knowledge of their nameless
        destiny.

                        II

Where are the good minds of past days, the unshorn?
Villon, to be sure, with his
saw-toothed will and testament? Erasmus
who praised folly and

Shakespeare who wrote so that
nq school man or churchman could sanction him without
revealing his own imbecility? Aristotle,
shrewd and alone, a onetime herb peddler?

They all, like Aristophanes, knew the clouds and
said next to nothing of the soul's flight
but kept their heads and died—
like Socrates, Plato's better self, unmoved.

Where? They live today in their old state because
of the pace they kept that keeps
them now fresh in our thoughts, their
relics, ourselves: Toulouse-Lautrec, the

deformed who lived in a brothel and painted
the beauty of whores. These were
the truth-tellers of whom we are the sole heirs
beneath the clouds that bring

shadow and darkness full of thought deepened
by rain against the clatter
of an empty sky. But anything to escape humanity!
Now it's spiritualism—again,

as if the certainty of a future life
were any solution to our dilemma: how to get
published not what we write but what we would write were
it not for the laws against libelous truth.

The poor brain unwilling to own the obtrusive body
would crawl from it like a crab and
because it succeeds, at times, in doffing that,
by its wiles of drugs or other "ecstasies," thinks

at last that it is quite free—exulted, scurrying to
some slightly larger shell some snail
has lost (where it will live). And so, thinking,
pretends a mystery! an unbodied

thing that would still be a brain—but no body,
something that does not eat but flies by the propulsions
of pure—what? into the sun itself, illimitedly
and exists so forever, blest, washed, purged

and at ease in non-representational bursts
of shapeless flame, sentient (naturally!)—and keeps
touch with the earth (by former works) at least.
The intellect leads, leads still! Beyond the clouds.

III

(Scherzo)

I came upon a priest once at St. Andrew's
in Amalfi in crimson and gold brocade riding
the clouds of his belief.

It happened that we tourists had intervened
at some mid-moment of the ritual—
tipped the sacristan or whatever it was.

No one else was there—porphyry and alabaster,
the light flooding in scented
with sandalwood—but this holy man

jiggling upon his buttocks to the litany
chanted, in response, by two kneeling altar boys!
I was amazed and stared in such manner

that he, caught half off the earth
in his ecstasy—though without losing a beat—
turned and grinned at me from his cloud.

IV

With each, dies a piece of the old life, which he carries,
a precious burden, beyond! Thus each
is valued by what he carries and that is his soul—
diminishing the bins by that much
unless replenished.

It is that which is the brotherhood:
the old life, treasured. But if they live?
What then?

The clouds remain
—the disordered heavens, ragged, ripped by winds
or dormant, a caligraphy of scaly dragons and bright moths,
of straining thought, bulbous or smooth,
ornate, the flesh itself (in which
the poet foretells his own death); convoluted, lunging upon
a pismire, a conflagration, a . . . .

Ballad of Faith

Ballad of Faith

No dignity without chromium
No truth but a glossy finish
If she purrs she's virtuous
If she hits ninety she's pure

ZZZZZZZZZ!
Step on the gas, brother
(the horn sounds hoarsely)

And Who Do You Think "They" Are?

The day when the under-cover writings
of the Russians are in, that day
we'll have an anthology, all around,
to knock their heads off.

War will grow sick, puke its guts
and if, dog-like, it wants to lick up
that, let it (after we have
put poison in it) for good and all.

The Non-Entity

The rusty-gold green trees
cone-shaped, animadvertent
cissiform, cramped

—a maple solitary
upon the wood's face. Behind
it an ocean roars, rocks

the mind, janistically
pours autumn, shaking nerves
of color over it

Childe Harold to the Round Tower Came

Obviously, in a plutocracy
the natural hero
is the man who robs a bank

Look at him, the direct eyes,
the forehead! Clearly
he is intelligent—but

with humor. Half suppressed
it leaps from his eyes
crinkling the skin under them.

His face has two sides,
brows that bespeak courage—
directed by research, that

purple word of the elite!
And love! bulbous (in
the lower lip) with desire

as in all full blooded
creatures at their best, affec-
tionate but alas, guarded to

survive. To survive is
the crown of virtue in this
world of finance. He will be

groined like a manager,
but more humane, the eyes
bluer, he will have

a more piercing look, greater
dash, be more freehanded
—the face deeper lined.

What *must* he be who is
their master? makes them shake,
steel themselves against

him at great cost, a whole
fleet of armored trucks, in
which, snails, oh what

poverty of means lies encased
there to insure
against his bounty . . .

Io Baccho!

God created alcohol
and it wasn't privately for the Russians
God created alcohol
and it wasn't for Dr. Goldsmith

It was for Mrs. Reiter
who is bored with having children
though she loves them.
God created alcohol to release
and engulf us. Shall I
say it is the only evidence of God
in this environment?

Mrs. R. doesn't drink
but I drink and I told the angel,
God created alcohol!
—if it weren't for that I'd say
there wasn't Any—
thinking of Mrs. R. who is
one eighth American Indian
and what with the pain in her guts
stands like an Indian
"If I had the strength"
Why should I bother to tell you?

God created alcohol
Shall I swoon like Mr. Keats?
and not from looking
at a Grecian urn. God created alcohol
to allay us

The Centenarian

I don't think we shall
any of us live as long as
has she, we haven't the
steady mind and strong heart—

Wush a deen a daddy O
There's whisky in the jar!

I wish you could have seen
her yesterday
with her red cheeks and
snow-white hair
so cheerful and contented—
she was a picture—

We sang hymns for her.

She couldn't join us but
when we had done she raised
her hands and clapped them
softly together.

Then when I brought her
her whisky and water I said
to her as we always do—

Wush a deen a daddy O
There's whisky in the jar!

She couldn't say the first
part but she managed to
repeat at the end—

There's whisky in the jar!

All That Is Perfect in Woman

All That Is Perfect in Woman

The symbol of war, a war
fast accomplished
flares in all our faces
an alcoholic flame—

Miami sunlight:
the pattern of waves
mottled with foam
against a blond day!

The fish scream
in soundless agony
trapped by its
sulphuric acid—

a blow-torch flame
at exorbitant cost
virginity
longing for snow and

a quiet life
that will (rightly)
blossom as
a mangled corpse:

Our own Joppolo Schmidt
the G.I. Joe
acted by himself,
a pathetic scene laid

upon thin slices
of sympathy, a snack
between halves
to rouse a smile.

And in our mouths!
a foot minus three toes—
In our embraces

a head partly scorched,
hairless and with
no nose! Between

the thighs a delicious
lung with entrails
and a tongue or gorget!

Blithe spirit! Monody
with feces—you
must sing of her and

behold the overpowering
foetor of her
girlish breasts and breath:

tumbled seas,
washing waves, the grave's
grandfather.

Let us praise! praise
the dreadful symbol of
carnivorous sex—

The gods live!
severally amongst us—
This is their familiar!

—whose blue eyes
and laughing mouth affirm
the habeas corpus
of our resignation

Oh Lorca, Lorca—
shining singer if you
could have been
alive for this!

At five in the afternoon.

—fecund and jocund
are familiar to the sea
and what dangles, lacerant,
under the belly of
the Portuguese Man O'War is also
familiar to the sea, familiar
to the sea, the sea.

The Rat

The Rat

The rat sits up and works his
    moustaches, the ontologic
phenomenon of cheese rifting his
    blood to orgiastic rule.

The tail, epicene in its application,
    the round-file tail,
that fearsome appendage which man
    for all his zest

cannot match—other than conceptu-
    ally, of which his
most thought latterly consists.
    How like this man

the rat is in the ubiquity of his
    deformity: plague
infected fleas come, through
    the connivance of

the San Frigando Chamber of
    Commerce, to infest the very
gophers of Nevada. His wise
    eyes mewing in his

spindle head the rat thrives, well
    suited to a world
conditioned to such human "tropism
    for order" at all cost.

Jingle

There ought to be a wedding
a wedding, a wedding!
There ought to be a wedding
between Russia and the United States

There'd be some pretty children
some children, some children
There'd be some pretty children
to cheer the world along

The classes liquidated
liquidated, liquidated
the rich would be supplanted
by the meek enriched by love

And we'd vote the tyrant under
tyrant under, tyrant under
by a landslide, by a landslide
when we would. We would, we would!

Every Day

Every day that I go out to my car
I walk through a garden
and wish often that Aristotle
had gone on
to a consideration of the dithyrambic
poem—or that his notes had survived

Coarse grass mars the fine lawn
as I look about right and left
tic toc—
And right and left the leaves
upon the yearling peach grow along
the slender stem

No rose is sure. Each is one rose
and this, unlike another,
opens flat, almost as a saucer without
a cup. But it is a rose, rose
pink. One can feel it turning slowly
upon its thorny stem

The Unfrocked Priest

1

When a man had gone
up
in Russia from a small
town
to the University
he
returned a hero—
people
bowed down to him—
his
ego, nourished by this,
mount-
ed to notable works.

2

Here
in the streets the kids
say
Hello Pete! to me—
What
can one be or
imagine?
Nothing is reverenced
nothing
looked up to. What
can
come of that sort of
dis-
respect for the under-
standing?

For G.B.S., Old

As the mind burns
the external is swallowed
nor can cold
censor it when it launches
its attack

Sever man
into his parts of bird and fish
Wake him
to the plausibilities
of those changes
he contemplates but does not dare

And by such acceptance
he forfeits
the green perspectives
which frightened him off
to his own destruction—

the mirage
the shape of a shape
become the shape he feared
his Tempest frozen
into a pattern
of ice.

The Words, the Words, the Words

The perfume of the iris, sweet citron,
is enhanced by money, the
odor of buckwheat, the woman's odor.
Sand does not chafe, with money.
Sheep fold, horse neigh but money
mollifies it.
Leap or swim
sleep or be drunk in whatever arms
or none
money is the crown

Your eyes, thighs, breasts—rose pointed,
money is their couch, their room,
the light from between lattices . . .

Lady behind the hedge, behind the
wall:
silken limbs, white brow,
money filters in through the shelving
leaves over you

Rise and shake your skirts
to the buttercups, yellow as polished
gold

Lustspiel

Vienna the Volk iss very lustig,
she makes no sorry for anything!
        She likes to dance and sing!

Vienna is a brave city, the girls
have sturdy legs. Yeah!
        She likes to dance and sing!

Death conquered Vienna but his men
had to be called off because
given the meanest break she'd lead
them hellbent to chuck the racket
for there's not a soul in Vienna
        but likes to dance and sing!

—drop their guns, dump the boss
grab a girl and join the rest
        who like to dance and sing!

Vienna the Volk iss very lustig,
she makes no sorry for anything!
        She likes to dance and sing!

April Is the Saddest Month

There they were
stuck
dog and bitch
halving the compass

Then when
with his yip
they parted
oh how frolicsome

she grew before him
playful
dancing and
how disconsolate

he retreated
hang-dog
she following
through the shrubbery

To Be Hungry Is to Be Great

The small, yellow grass-onion,
spring's first green, precursor
to Manhattan's pavements, when
plucked as it comes, in bunches,
washed, split and fried in
a pan, though inclined to be
a little slimy, if well cooked
and served hot on rye bread
is to beer a perfect appetizer—
and the best part
of it is they grow everywhere.

The Complexity

Strange that their dog
should look like the woman:
the eyes close together
the jowls prominent. But
the man loves the dog too,
an area curious in its
resemblance to that other,
a pleasant change
from the woman. Volpe
the man's name is. Wolf he
calls himself, a kindly
fellow who sells Italian
goat cheese . . .

A Note

When the cataract dries up, my dear
all minds attend it.
There is nothing left. Neither sticks
nor stones can build it up again
nor old women with their rites of green twigs

Bending over the remains, a body
struck through the breast bone
with a sharp spear—they have borne him
to an ingle at the wood's edge
from which all maidenhood is shent

—though he roared
once the cataract is dried up and done.
What rites can do to keep alive
the memory of that flood they will do
then bury it, old women that they are,
secretly where all male flesh is buried.

Drugstore Library

That's the kind of books
they read.
They love their filth.
Knee boots
and they want to hear
it suck
when they pull 'em out

The R R Bums

Their most prized possession—
their liberty—
         Hands behind a coat
shiny green. Tall, the eyes
downcast—
       Sunlight through a clutter of
wet clouds, lush weeds—
              The oriole!
Hungry as an oriole.

Choral: the Pink Church

Choral: the Pink Church

Pink as a dawn in Galilee
whose stabbing fingers routed
Aeschylus and murder blinked . . .

—and tho' I remember little
    as names go,
the thrust of that first light
    was to me
    as through a heart
    of jade—
as chinese as you please
but not by that—remote

Now,
    the Pink Church
        trembles
to the light (of dawn) again,
    rigors of more
    than sh'd wisely
    be said at one stroke,
singing!
        Covertly.
            Subdued.

    Sing!
transparent to the light
    through which the light
shines, through the stone,
    until
the stone-light glows,
    pink jade
—that is the light and is
    a stone

and is a church—if the image
    hold . . .

as at a breath a face glows
    and fades!
Come all ye aberrant,
    drunks, prostitutes,
    Surrealists—
    Gide and—
Proust's memory (in a cork
    diving suit
looking under the sea
        of silence)
to bear witness:

Man is not sinful . . . unless
    he sin!
—Poe, Whitman, Baudelaire
    the saints
        of this calendar.

Oh ladies whose beds
    your
husbands defile! man, man
    is the bringer
    of pure delights
    to you!

Who else?

    And there stand
    the-banded-together
    in the name of
    the Philosophy Dep'ts

wondering at the nature

of the stuff
poured into
the urinals
of custom . . .

O Dewey! (John)
O James! (William)
O Whitehead!
teach well!
—above and beyond
your teaching stands
the Pink Church:
the nipples of
a woman who never
bore a
child . . .

Oh what new vows shall
we swear to make all swearing
futile:
the fool
the mentally deranged
the suicide?

—suckled of its pink delight

And beyond them all whine
the slaughtered, the famished
and the lonely—
the holy church of
their minds singing madly
in tune, its stones
sibilant and roaring—

Soft voiced . . .

To which, double bass:

A torch to a heap
    of new branches
    under the tied feet of
    Michael Servitus:

          Be ye therefore perfect
          even as your
          Father in Heaven
          is perfect

And all you liveried bastards,
    all (tho' pardon me
    all you who come
    rightly under that holy
    term)

          Harken!

—perfect as the pink and
    rounded breasts of a virgin!
Scream it in
          their stupid ears—
plugged by wads of
newspulp—

          Joy! Joy!
          —out of Elysium!

—chanted loud as a chorus from
    the Agonistes—

Milton, the unrhymer,
          singing among
              the rest . . .

like a Communist.

Incognito

Incognito

I want to be where Fordie is
(Bury my face in the dirt
—like a Maori, those

who slash their faces
with knives, carving new lips,
a nose dismembered

the cheeks scar-coils,
the forehead seamed—to
live (for such a face is

incognito, the man gone)
like Fordie, no man now but
an art for Cherubim

and Seraphim to reface
with words, intaglio. There
Fordie sings to the harp, sighing.

3 A.M.
The Girl with the Honey Colored Hair

Everyone looked and, passing, revealed
himself
by the light of her hair heavy
upon her shoulders

—the haggard drunk
holding onto the backs of the seats,
face tense of a fixed purpose
toward the toilet

—the savage-looking female wearing
a picture hat and
mascara, hard eyes. And the two
colored women:

an older in a small beret and a younger
in slicked glossy hair
sitting,
for protection and with side-

long looks, close to her friend—all
were affected as she
turned frightened to address
me, pitifully alone.

A Crystal Maze

Hard, hard to learn—
that love, through bars and against
back strokes, is to make mine
each by his own gesture—the toss
of a cigarette—
giving, laying himself bare,
offering, watching
for its flash of certainty in
the confused onslaught—

—that any one is not one
but twenty—twelve men, two women
a hidden positive and a visible
deception—

Take it, black curls clustered in
the hollow of the neck, unwilling
to be released for less—
laying desperately with impeccable
composure an unnecessary
body clean to the eye—

And emerge curiously changed—
amazement in that loveliness
about the perfect breasts
Venus, her way, close sister to
the martyr—each his own way

One avidly sheathing the flesh—
one denying it. One loosed through
the gone brain of an old man—

Pity has no part in it—

Loosed to take its course, love
is the master—and the variable
certainty in the crosses of
uncertainty—
                    the flesh, therewith,
a quietness—
and quieted—standing asserted

11

Hard, hard to learn—
that love, against bars and
counter strokes is mine,
each by his own gesture—
the toss of a cigarette—
laying himself bare
offering, watching
for a flash of certainty
in the confused onslaught—

That one is not one
but—twelve, two women,
a hidden positive and
a visible deception—

Take it! black curls clustered
in the hollow of the neck
laying desperately with
impeccable composure
an uncalled for body clean
to the eye—

                    and emerging

curiously changed—
amazement in that loveliness
about the perfect breasts—
the flesh thereto
a quietness and
quieted, standing asserted

New Mexico

Anger can be transformed
to a kitten—as love
may become a mountain in
the disturbed mind, the
mind that prances like
a horse or nibbles, starts
and stares in the parched
sage of the triple
world—of stone, stone
layered and beaten under
the confessed brilliance
of this desert noon.

Seafarer

The sea will wash in
but the rocks—jagged ribs
riding the cloth of foam
or a knob or pinnacles
    with gannets—
are the stubborn man.

He invites the storm, he
lives by it! instinct
with fears that are not fears
but prickles of ecstasy,
a secret liquor, a fire
that inflames his blood to
coldness so that the rocks
seem rather to leap
at the sea than the sea
to envelope them. They strain
forward to grasp ships
or even the sky itself that
bends down to be torn
upon them. To which he says,
It is I! I who am the rocks!
Without me nothing laughs.

The Sound of Waves

A quatrain? Is that
the end I envision?
Rather the pace
which travel chooses.

Female? Rather the end
of giving and receiving
—of love: love surmounted
is the incentive.

Hardly. The incentive
is nothing surmounted,
the challenge lying
     elsewhere.

No end but among words
looking to the past,
plaintive and unschooled,
wanting a discipline

But wanting
more than discipline
a rock to blow upon
as a mist blows

or rain is driven
against some
headland jutting into
a sea—with small boats

perhaps riding under it
while the men fish
there, words blowing in
taking the shape of stone

.　　.　　.　　.　　.

Past that, past the image:
a voice!
out of the mist
above the waves and

the sound of waves, a
voice　　　.　　speaking!

Venus over the Desert

If I do not sin, she said, you shall not
walk in long gowns down stone corridors.
There is no reprieve where there is no fall-
ing off. I lie in your beds all night, from
me you wake and go about your tasks. My flesh
clings to your bones. What use is holiness
unless it affirm my perfections, my breasts,
my thighs which you part, shaking, and my lips
the door to my pleasures? Sin, you call it,
but there cannot be cold unless the heat
has bred it, how can you know otherwise? Love
comfort me in the face of my defeats! Poor
monks, you think you are gentle but I tell you
you kill as sure as shot kills a bird flying.

Mists over the River

The river-mirror mirrors the cold sky
through mists that tangle sunlight,
the sunlight of early morning,
in their veils veiling

the dark outlines of the shores. But
the necessity, you say, cries
aloud for the adjusting—greater than
song greater perhaps than all song

While the song, self committed, the river
a mirror swathed in sunlight
the river in its own body cries out
also, silently

from its obscuring veils. You
insist on my unqualified endorsement.
Many years, I see, many years
of reading have not made you wise.

"I Would Not Change for Thine"

Shall I stroke your thighs,
having eaten?
Shall I kiss you,
having drunk?

Or drink to you only

—leaving the poor soul
who lives with her husband
(the truck driver)
three months, to spend
the next six
where she can find it,
dropping the kid
of that abandon in whatever
hospital about the country
will take her?

(both have T.B.)

What course has she
to offer at her academy
that he returns to her
each year to listen,
repeated, to the lectures
of her adventures?
And having drunk avidly
and eaten of the philosophies
of their reunion
—tells her his own . ?

Happy, happy married pair

I should come to you
fasting, my sweet—you
to whom I would send
a rosy wreath not so much
honoring thee as lending it
a hope that there
I might remembered be.

The Pause

Values are split, summer, the fierce
jet an axe would not sever, spreads out
at length, of its own weight, a rainbow
over the lake of memory—the hard
stem of pure speed broken. Autumn
comes, fruit of many contours, that
glistening tegument painters love hiding
the soft pulp of the insidious reason,
dormant, for worm to nibble or for woman.
But there, within the seed, shaken by
fear as by a sea, it wakes again! to
drive upward, presently, from that soft
belly such a stem as will crack quartz.

Mama

Kitten! Kitten! grown woman!
you curl into the pillows
to make a man clamp his jaws
for tenderness over you   .

stroking, stroking, the nerves
taut, alert for the swift
counter-slap will make him (you
shall see) bear down hard.

The Love Charm

Take this, the nexus
of unreality,
my head, I detach
it for you. Take it

in your hands, metal
to eat out
the heart, if held
to the heart. Hold it

to your heart
and wait, only wait
the while
its fissions curdle.

Approach to a City

Getting through with the world—
I never tire of the mystery
of these streets: the three baskets
of dried flowers in the high

bar-room window, the gulls wheeling
above the factory, the dirty
snow—the humility of the snow that
silvers everything and is

trampled and lined with use—yet
falls again, the silent birds
on the still wires of the sky, the blur
of wings as they take off

together. The flags in the heavy
air move against a leaden
ground—the snow
pencilled with the stubble of old

weeds: I never tire of these sights
but refresh myself there
always for there is small holiness
to be found in braver things.

Song

If I
could count the silence
I could sleep, sleep.

But it
is one, one. No head even
to gnaw. Spinning.

If I
could halt the glazed
spinning, surface of glass,

my mind
could shove in its fingers
and break apart

the smooth
singleness of the night—
until sleep dropped as rain

upon me.

A Rosebush in an Unlikely Garden

The flowers are yours
the full blown
the half awakened
yours

who fished heads
and arms on D day in a net
from the bloody
river

The stillness
of this squalid corner this
veined achievement is
yours

The Lion

Traffic, the lion, the sophisticate,
facing the primitive, alabaster,
the new fallen snow
stains its chastity the new shade

Use defames! the attack disturbs our sleep

This is the color of the road, the color
of the lion, sand color

—to follow the lion, of use or usage,
even to church! the bells achime
above the fallen snow!

—all follow the same road, space.

The Lion

Winter, the churned snow, the lion
flings the woman, taking her
by the throat upon his gullied
shoulders—shaking the weight fast
and unmolested plunges with her
among the trees—where the whiteness
sparkles—to devour her there:
transit to uses: where the traffic
mounts, a chastity packed with lewdness,
a rule, dormant, against the loosely
fallen snow—the thick muscles
working under the skin, the head
like a tree-stump, gnawing: chastity
to employment, lying down bloodied
to bed together for the last time.

An Eternity

Come back, Mother, come back from
the dead—not to "Syria," not there
but hither—to this place.

You are old, Mother, old
and almost cold, come back from
the dead—where I cannot yet join you.
Wait awhile, wait a little while.
Like Todhunter
let us give up rhyme. This
winter moonlight is a bitter thing,
I like it no better than you do.
Let us wait
for some darker moment of the moon.

At ninety the strangeness of death
is upon you. I have been to all
corners of the mind. What gift
can I bring you but luxury and that
you have taught me to despise. I
turn my face to the wall,
revert to my beginnings and turn
my face also to the wall.

And yet, Mother, that isn't true.
—the night, the night we face
is black but of no more weight than
the day—the day we faced and were
defeated and yet lived
to face the night in which
the fair moon shines—its continents
visible to the naked eye! Naked
is a good word in that context

—makes the night light! light as
a feather (in the night!)

The soul, my dear, is paramount,
the soul of things
that makes the dead moon shine.

Frankly, I do not love you.

All I can see (by the moon's flame)
whatever answer
there may be otherwise, *that* we know,
is abandoned

I remember how at eighty-five
you battled through the crisis and
             survived!

I suppose, in fact I know,
you've never heard of Shapley—
an astronomer. Now there's a man—
the best   .   .

             Not like Flamarion,
your old favorite, who wanted
to popularize astronomy, Shapley's
not like Flamarion

             You preceded him.

It is the loveless soul, the soul
of things that has surpassed
our loves. In this—you live,
Mother, live in me   .
                          always.

The Three Graces

We have the picture of you in mind,
when you were young, posturing
(for a photographer) in scarves
(if you could have done it) but now,
for none of you is immortal, ninety-
three, the three, ninety and three,
Mary, Ellen and Emily, what
beauty is it clings still about you?
Undying? Magical? For there is still
no answer, why we live or why
you will not live longer than I
or that there should be an answer why
any should live and whatever other
should die. Yet you live. You live
and all that can be said is that
you live, time cannot alter it—
and as I write this Mary has died.

The Horse Show

Constantly near you, I never in my entire
sixty-four years knew you so well as yesterday
or half so well. We talked. You were never
so lucid, so disengaged from all exigencies
of place and time. We talked of ourselves,
intimately, a thing never heard of between us.
How long have we waited? almost a hundred years.

You said, Unless there is some spark, some
spirit we keep within ourselves, life, a
continuing life's impossible—and it is all
we have. There is no other life, only the one.
The world of the spirits that comes afterward
is the same as our own, just like you sitting
there they come and talk to me, just the same.

They come to bother us. Why? I said. I don't
know. Perhaps to find out what we are doing.
Jealous, do you think? I don't know. I
don't know why they should want to come back.
I was reading about some men who had been
buried under a mountain, I said to her, and
one of them came back after two months,

digging himself out. It was in Switzerland,
you remember? Of course I remember. The
villagers tho't it was a ghost coming down
to complain. They were frightened. They
do come, she said, what you call
my "visions." I talk to them just as I
am talking to you. I see them plainly.

Oh if I could only read! You don't know
what adjustments I have made. All
I can do is to try to live over again
what I knew when your brother and you
were children—but I can't always succeed.
Tell me about the horse show. I have
been waiting all week to hear about it.

Mother darling, I wasn't able to get away.
Oh that's too bad. It was just a show;
they make the horses walk up and down
to judge them by their form. Oh is that
all? I tho't it was something else. Oh
they jump and run too. I wish you had been
there, I was so interested to hear about it.

The Birth of Venus

The Birth of Venus

Today small waves are rippling, crystal clear, upon the
    pebbles
at Villefranche whence from the wall, at the Parade Grounds
    of
the Chasseurs Alpins, we stood and watched them; or pass-
    ing along
the cliff on the ledge between the sea and the old fortress,
    heard
the long swell stir without cost among the rock's teeth. But
    we

are not there!—as in the Crimea the Black Sea is blue with
    waves
under a smiling sky, or be it the Labrador North Shore, or
    wherever
else in the world you will, the world of indolence and April;
    as,
November next, spring will enliven the African coast south-
    ward
and we not there, not there, not there!

Why not believe that we shall be young again? Surely
    nothing
could be more to our desire, more pebble-plain under a
    hand's breath
wavelet, a jeweled thing, a Sapphic bracelet, than this.
    Murder
staining the small waves crimson is not more moving—
    though we strain
in our minds to make it so, and stare.

Cordite, heavy shells falling on the fortifications of Se-
    bastopol,

189

fired by the Germans first, then by the Russians, are in-
   different to
our agony—as are small waves in the sunlight. But we need
   not elect
what we do not desire. Torment, in the daisied fields before
   Troy
or at Amiens or the Manchurian plain is not

of itself the dearest desired of our world. We do not have
   to die,
in bitterness and the most excruciating torture, to feel! We
   can
lean on the wall and experience an ecstasy of pain, if pain it
   must
be, but a pain of love, of dismemberment if you will, but a
   pain
of almond blossoms, an agony of mimosa trees in bloom, a

scented cloud! Even, as old Ford would say, an exquisite
   sense of
viands. Would there be no sculpture, no painting, no Pintu-
   ricchio, no
Botticelli—or frescos on the jungle temples of Burma (that
   the jungles
have reclaimed) or Picasso at Cannes but for war? Would
   there be
no voyages starting from the dunes at Huelva

over the windy harbor? No Seville cathedral? Possibly so.
   Even
the quietness of flowers is perhaps deceptive. But why must
   we suffer
ourselves to be so torn to sense our world? Or believe we
   must so
suffer to be born again? Let the homosexuals seduce whom
   they will

under what bushes along the coasts of the Middle Sea

rather than have us insist on murder. Governments are
      defeats, distor-
tions. I wish (and so I fail). Notwithstanding, I wish we
      might
learn of an April of small waves—deadly as all slaughter,
      that we
shall die soon enough, to dream of April, not knowing why
      we have been
struck down, heedless of what greater violence.

14 New Poems (1950)

May 1st Tomorrow

The mind's a queer sponge
                squeeze it and out come bird songs
small leaves highly enameled
                and . moments of good reading
(rapidly) *Tuck, tuck, tuck, tuck, tuck!*
                —the mind remembering .
Not, *not* in flux (that diarrhoea)
                but nesting. *Chee woo! Tuck!*
the male mind, nesting: glancing up
                from a letter from a friend
asking . the mind
                to be . squeezed and let
him be the liquor which, when
                we release it, *he* shall be sopped
up, *all* his weight, and
                released again . by squeezing.

Full, it moulds itself . . .
                like a brown breast, full
not of milk but of what breasts are
                to the eye, hemispherical
(2 would make a sphere)
                to the mind; a view of the mind
that, in a way, gives milk:
                that liquor that minds
feed upon. To feed, to feed *now*!
                Chuck, chuck, chuck. Toe whee. Chuck!
—burdensome as twin stones
                that the mind alone can milk
and give again .
                Chee woo! etcetera

Après le Bain

I gotta
buy me a new
girdle.

(I'll buy
you one) O.K.
(I wish

you'd wig-
gle that way
for me,

I'd be
a happy man)
I GOTTA

wig-
gle for *this*.
(You pig)

Spring Is Here Again, Sir.

Goffle brook of a May day
(*Mon cher Cocteau*
qui déjeune des fois
avec Picasso) blossoms
in the manner of antiquity

Which is an obliquity
for the movement
and the sheen of ripples
bridging the gap for
age-old winnowing decay—

from then to now. Which
leaves very little
but the sun and air
unless one should prefer
a pool of human spittle

over which to grieve.
Rhyme it regularly if you
will. I say the night
is not always gay for
an old man who has sinned.

But the brook! is mine
and I must still prefer it
to the summits of Thibet
from which to take off:
—of spring, to the air

for relief! smell of clover,
cherries are ripening.
We lay, Floss and I, on
the grass together, in
the warm air: a bird flew

into a bush, dipped our
hands in the running water—
cold, too cold; but found
it, to our satisfaction,
as in the past, still wet.

The Hard Core of Beauty

The most marvellous is not
                        the beauty, deep as that is,
but the classic attempt
                        at beauty,
at the swamp's center: the
                        dead-end highway, abandoned
when the new bridge went in finally.
                        There, either side an entry
from which, burned by the sun,
                        the paint is peeling—
two potted geraniums .
                        Step inside: on a wall, a
painted plaque showing
                        ripe pomegranates .
—and, leaving, note
                        down the road—on a thumbnail,
you could sketch it on a thumbnail—
                        stone steps climbing
full up the front to
                        a second floor
minuscule
                        portico
peaked like the palate
                        of a child! God give us again
such assurance.
                        There are
                        rose bushes either side
this entrance and plum trees
                        (one dead) surrounded
at the base by worn-out auto-tire
                        casings! for what purpose
but the glory of the Godhead

                        that poked
her twin shoulders, supporting
                        the draggled blondness
of her tresses, from beneath
                        the patient waves.
And we? the whole great world abandoned
                        for nothing at all, intact,
the lost world of symmetry
                        and grace: bags of charcoal
piled deftly under
                        the shed at the rear, the
ditch at the very rear a passageway
                        through the mud,
triumphant! to pleasure,
                        pleasure; pleasure by boat,
a by-way of a Sunday
                        to the smooth river.

Tolstoy

          That art is evil (stale
          art, he might have said)
          was to his mind as weevil
          to the cotton-head

          Stale art, like stale fish
          stinks (I might have said)
          You are ageing, Master
          Commit yourself to Heaven

Cuchulain

I had been his fool
    not a dog
    not his murderer

To court war which I
    redreamed
    —he suffered

To force him backward
    into the sea
    blood of his blood

Blood of my blood in
    tortured
    bewilderment

—his fool, shrewd witted
    to protect
    and beguile him

To read rather
    that which I
    suffered

Not a morose pig
    his doom
    to escape only

My fate—take
    upon myself
    the kindler, the

Match-man, the mind
    miner, the very
    woman

His life lived in
    me warmed
    at his fires

A power in the night.
    Madman, clown—
    success

Twelve Line Poem

Pitiful lovers broken by your loves
the head of a man
the parts disjointed of a woman
unshaved pushing forward

And you? Withdrawn caressive
the thighs limp eyes
filling with tears the lower lip
trembling, why do you try

so hard to be a man? You are
a lover! Why adopt
the reprehensible absurdities of
an inferior attitude?

Nun's Song

For the wrongs that women do
we dedicate ourselves, O God, to You
and beg You to believe
that we truly grieve.

Our defects, not fear,
drive us to seek to be so very near
Your loving tenderness
that You may bless

us everlastingly; not dread,
but risen from the sorry dead
that each may be, at Your side
a very bride!

The Self

The poem
is a discipline
What you need
to sober you
is what you have

Your children

Let them
children
teach you

the peach flower
the grape
globular locks
curling pathetically about
the temples
their eyes
their rosy cheeks

the poem
laid crudely
delicately
before you.

Another Old Woman

If I could keep her
here, near me
I'd fill her mind
with my thoughts

She would get
their complexion
and live again. But
I could not live

along with her
she would drain me
as sand drains
water. Visions pos-

sess her. Dreams
unblooded walk
her mind. Her mind
does not faint.

Throngs visit her:
We are at war
with Mexico—to
please her fancy—

A cavalry column
is deploying
over a lifeless terrain
—to impress us!

She describes it
her face bemused—
alert to details. They
ride without saddles

tho' she is ig-
norant of the word
"bareback," but knows
accurately that I

am not her son, now,
but a stranger
listening. She
breaks off, her looks

intent, bent
inward, with a curious
glint to her eyes:
They say that

when the fish comes!
(gesture of getting
a strike) it
is a great joy!

Wide Awake, Full of Love

Being in this stage
I look to the last,
see myself returning:
the seamed face
as of a tired rider
upon a tired horse
coming up . . .

What of your dish-eyes
that have seduced
me? Your voice
whose cello notes
upon the theme have led
me to the music?

I see your neck scrawny
your thighs worn
your hair thinning,
whose round brow
pushes it aside, and
turn again upon
the thought: To migrate

to that South to hop
again upon the shining
grass there
half ill with love
and mope and
will not startle for
the grinning worm

Song

Pluck the florets from
a clover head
and suck the honey, sweet.
The world
will realign itself—ex-
cluding Russia
and the U.S.A. and planes
run soon
by atomic power defying
gravity.
Pluck the florets from
a clover head
and suck the honey, sweet.

Song

Russia! Russia! you might say
and furrow the brow
but I say: There are flowers upon
the R.R. embankment
woven by growing in and out among
the rusted guard cables
lying there in the grass, flowers
daisy shaped, pink
and white in this September glare.
Count upon it there
will be soon a further revolution.

Convivio

We forget sometimes that no matter what
our quarrels we are the same brotherhood:
the rain falling or the rain withheld,
—berated by women, barroom smells
or breath of Persian roses! our wealth
is words. And when we go down to defeat,
before the words, it is still within and
the concern of, first, the brotherhood.
Which should quiet us, warm and arm us
besides to attack, always attack—but to
reserve our worst blows for the enemy, those
who despise the word, flout it, stem,
leaves and root; the liars who decree laws
with no purpose other than to make a screen
of them for larceny, murder—for our
murder, we who salute the word and would
have it clean, full of sharp movement.

Two Pendants: for the Ears

The Lesson

The hydrangea
pink cheeked nods its head
a paper brain
without a skull

a brain intestined
to the invisible root
where
beside the rose and acorn

thought lies communal
with
the brooding worm
True but the air

remains
the wanton the dancing
that
holding enfolds it

a flower
aloof
Flagrant as a flag
it shakes that seamy head

or
snaps it drily
from the anchored stem
and sets it rolling

Two Pendants: for the Ears

I

The particulars of morning are more to be desired
than night's vague images.

I dreamed of a tiger, wounded,
lying broken
upon a low parapet
                    at least they said
it was a tiger though I never
saw it—more than a shadow—
for the night:

                    an open plaza
before the post-office
—but very obscure

            When I arrived
the people were underground
huddled into a group and terrified
from the recent happenings:

a terrific fight, apparently—
between the beast and
a man, its trainer, lying
he also, out there now
horribly wounded—perhaps dead
or exhausted
—during a lull of the encounter,
having defended himself well
                    —and bleeding.

No one knew or exactly knew
how the immediate
situation lay.

               Thoughtlessly or at least
without thought, my instinct
took me toward the man. I walked
into the darkness
toward the scene of the fight.

Somewhat to the right
apparently unable to lift itself
and hanging upon
the stone wall, I seemed
to make out the beast and could
hear it panting, heavily

         At the same moment,
to the left, on the ground under
the wall, I saw, or
rather heard, the man—or
what I took to be the man. He was
mewing softly, a spasmodic
high pitched sighing—probably
unconscious.

              As I got half way out
from the people huddled back of me
to the scene of the conflict
the breathing of the beast stopped
as though the better
for him to listen and I could feel
him watching me.

          I paused.

                                     I could
                make out nothing clearly and then
                did the logical thing: unarmed
                I saw that I was helpless and so
                turned and walked back to the others.

                Has no one notified the police?
                I said.

                That was the end of the dream.

                                The yard
                                from the bathroom window
                                is another matter:

                                Here everything
                                is clear. The wind
                                sounds, I can make out

                                the yellow of the flowers—
                                For half an hour
                                I do not move.

                                It is Easter Sunday

                The short and brilliantly stabbing grass
                (my son went out during the night
                                and has not returned—later
                I found that he had returned and had
                fallen asleep on the couch downstairs—
                his bed was empty)
                —marked (plotted) by the squares
                and oblongs of the flower beds
                                (beds! beds for the flowers)
                the sticks of roses that will later show
                brilliant blooms stand out

A cloud
unclassic, a white unnamed cloud of
small tufts of white flowers
        light as wishes
(later to give place to red berries
        called service berries)
—a cloud through which the east sun
shines, anonymous
            (a tree marked
by the practical sense of my countrymen
the shad bush   .   to say
fish are in the river)

        floating

There are no girls here
        not above
           virtual infancy

—small white flowers
        shining
           profusely together

Thousands of glittering small leaves
that no church bell calls to Mass
—but there will be a mass soon
on the weighted branches

      —their smiles vanish
at the age of four. Later they
sob and throw their arms about my
waist, babies I have myself delivered
from their agonized mothers. They
sob and cling to me, their breasts heavy

217

with milk, pressing my coat and refuse
to let go until their sobs
quiet. Then they smile (at me) through
their tears. But it is only
for a moment—they soon become
women again.

The wind howled still at my
bedroom window but here, overlooking the
garden, I no longer hear its howls
nor see it moving   .

My thoughts
are like the distant smile of a child
who will (never) be a beautiful woman

like
the distant smile of a woman who
will say:
        —only to keep you a moment
longer. Oh I know I'm a stinker—

but

only to keep you, it's only
to keep you   .   a few moments

Let me have a cigarette.

The little flowers
got the names we might bestow now
upon drugs for headaches and obesity.
It is periwinkle time now.

How can you, my countrymen
            (what bathos

hangs about that title, unwarranted
in good measure but there: a fault
of art)
                    how can you permit yourselves
to be so cheated—your incomes
taken away and you, chromium
in your guts (rat poison)
                              until you are swollen
beyond all recognition

It is not in a return to the ideals
preserved for us
by primitive peoples that our society
will heal itself of its maladies

We read, after breakfast, Flossie,
our son and I—or rather I read to
them from a friendly poet's translations,
*Plato's Inscription for a Statue
of Pan* (I know no Greek)   He said:

Be still O green cliffs of the Dryads
Still O springs bubbling from the rocks
                              and be still
Many voiced crying of the ewes:
                              It is Pan
Pan with his sweet pipe:
                              the clever lips run
Over the withed reeds
                              while all about him
Rise from the ground to dance
                              with joyous tread
The nymphs of the water
                              nymphs of the oaken forest

—forgot   (baby)
            but it seems less
out of place than the present, all the
present for all that it is present
                        (baby)

The two or three young fruit trees,
even the old and battered watering can
of characteristic shape
                  (made to pour from the bottom)
are looking up at us   .   I
say "us" but I mean, alas, only me.

II

ELENA

You lean the head forward
and wave the hand,
with a smile,
twinkling the fingers
            I say to myself
            Now it is spring
            Elena is dying

What snows, what snow
enchained her—
she of the tropics
is melted
            now she is dying

The mango, the guava
long forgot for
apple and cherry
wave good-bye

                    now it is spring
                    Elena is dying
                        Good-bye

You think she's going to die?
said the old boy.
She's not going to die—not now.
In two days she'll be
all right again. When she dies
she'll

        If only she wouldn't
exhaust herself, broke in
the sturdy woman, his wife. She
fights so. You can't quieten her.

When she dies she'll go out
like a light. She's done it now
two or three times when
the wife's had her up, absolutely
out. But so far she's always
come out of it.
        Why just an hour ago
she sat up straight on that bed, as
straight as ever I saw her
in the last ten years, straight
as a ram-rod. You wouldn't believe
that would you? She's not
going to die   she'll be
raising Cain, looking for her grub
as per usual in the next two
or three days, you wait and see

Listen, I said, I met a man
last night told me what he'd brought
home from the market:

2 partridges
2 Mallard ducks
a Dungeness crab
24 hours out
of the Pacific
and 2 live-frozen
trout
from Denmark

What about that?

Elena is dying (I wonder)
willows and pear trees
whose encrusted branches
blossom all a mass
attend her on her way—

a guerdon
          (a garden)
              and cries of children
        indeterminate
Holy, holy, holy

                    (no ritual
but fact   .   in fact)

          until
the end of time (which is now)

How can you weep for her? I
cannot, I her son—though
I could weep for her without
compromising the covenant

          She will go alone.

—or pat to the times: go wept
by a clay statuette
          (if there be miracles)
a broken head of a small
St. Anne who wept at a kiss
from a child:
          She was so lonely

And Magazine #1 sues Magazine
#2, no less guilty—for libel
or infringement or dereliction
or confinement

Elena is dying (but perhaps
not yet)

Pis-en-lit attend her (I see
the children have been here)

Said Jowles, from under the
Ionian sea: What do you think
about that miracle, Doc?—that
little girl kissing
the head of that statue and making
it cry?

                    I hadn't
seen it.
              It's in the papers,
tears came out of the eyes.
I hope it doesn't turn
out to be something funny.

Let's see now: St. Anne
is the grandmother of Jesus. So
that makes St. Anne the mother

of the Virgin Mary

        M's a great letter, I confided.

What's that? So now it gets
to be Easter—you never know.

        Never. No, never.

The river, throwing off sparks
in a cold world

        Is this a private foight
            or kin I get into it?

This is a private fight.

        Elena is dying.
In her delirium she said
a terrible thing:

Who are you? NOW!
I, I, I, I stammered. I
am your son.

Don't go. I am unhappy.

About what? I said

About what is what.

The woman (who was watching)
added:
She thinks I'm her father.

Swallow it now: she wants
to do it herself.

　　　Let her spit.

At last! she said two days later
coming to herself and seeing me:

　　　—but I've been here
every day, Mother.

　　　　　　Well why don't
they put you where I can see you
then?

　　　She was crying this morning,
said the woman, I'm glad you came.

　　　　　　Let me clean your
glasses.

　　　　　　They put them on my nose!
They're trying to make a monkey
out of me.

　　　Were you thinking
of La Fontaine?

　　　　　　Can't you give me
something to make me disappear
completely, said she sobbing—but
completely!

　　　　　　No I can't do that
Sweetheart (You God damned belittling
fool, said I to myself)

There's a little Spanish wine,
pajarete
> p-a-j-a-r-e-t-e
But pure Spanish! I don't suppose
they have it any more.

(The woman started to move her)

But I have to see my child

Let me straighten you

I don't want the hand (my hand)
there (on her forehead)
—digging the nail of
her left thumb hard into my flesh,
the back of my own thumb
holding her hand   .   .   .

"If I had a dog ate meat
on Good Friday I'd kill him."
said someone off to the left

Then after three days:
I'm glad to see you up and doing,
said she to me brightly.

I told you she wasn't going to
die, that was just a remission,
I think you call it, said
the 3 day beard in a soiled
undershirt

I'm afraid I'm not much use
to you, Mother, said I feebly.
I brought you a bottle of wine

—a little late for Easter

Did you? What kind of wine?
A light wine?

Sherry.

What?

Jeres. You know, *jerez*. Here
                    (giving it to her)

So big! That will be my baby
now!
      (cuddling it in her arms)
Ave Maria Purissime! It is heavy!
I wonder if I could take
a little glass of it now?

                          Has
she eaten anything yet?

                          Has
she eaten anything yet!

Six oysters—she said
she wanted some fish and that's
all we had. A round
of bread and butter and a
banana

                      My God!

—two cups of tea and some
ice-cream.

Now she wants the wine.

Will it hurt her?

          No, I think
nothing will hurt her.

          She's
one of the wonders of the world
I think, said his wife.

          (To make the language
record it, facet to facet
not bored out—
          with an auger.

—to give also the unshaven,
          the rumblings of a
catastrophic past, a delicate
defeat—vivid simulations of
the mystery   .   )

We had leeks for supper, I said
What?

          Leeks! Hulda
gave them to me, they were going
to seed, the rabbits had
eaten everything else. I never
tasted better—from Pop's old
garden   .

          Pop's old what?

I'll have to clean out her ears

So my year is ended. Tomorrow
it will be April, the glory gone
the hard-edged light elapsed. Were
it not for the March within me,
the intensity of the cold sun, I
could not endure the drag
of the hours opposed to that weight,
the profusion to come later, that
comes too late. I have already
swum among the bars, the angular
contours, I have already lived
the year through

                Elena is dying

The canary, I said, comes and sits
on our table in the morning
at breakfast, I mean walks about
on the table with us there
and pecks at the table-cloth

                  He must
be a smart little bird

                Good-bye!

To Close

Will you please rush down and see
ma baby. You know, the one I talked
to you about last night

What was that?

Is this the baby specialist?

Yes, but perhaps you mean my son,
can't you wait until   .   ?

I, I, I don't think it's brEAthin'

The Rose

The Rose

The stillness of the rose
in time of war
reminds me of
the long sleep just begun
of that sparrow
his head pillowed unroughed
and unalarmed upon
the polished pavement or
of voluptuous hours
with some
breathless book when
stillness was an eternity
long since begun

The Visit

I have committed many errors
but I warn—the interplay
is not the tossed body. Though
the mind is subtler than the sea,
advancing at three speeds,
the fast, the medium and the slow,
recapitulating at every ninth
wave what was not at first directly
stated, that is still only
on the one level.

          There are the fish
and at the bottom, the ground,
no matter whether at five feet
or five miles, the ground, revealing,
when bared by the tides, living
barnacles, hungry on the rocks
as the mind is, that hiss as often
loudly when the sun bites them.

And I acknowledge, the mind is
still (though rarely) more than
its play. I can see also
the dagger in the left hand when
the right strikes. It does
not alter the case.

Let us resume. The
naive may be like a sunny day
deceptive
and is not to be despised
because it is so amusing to see
the zigzag and slender gulls

dip
into the featureless surface.
It is fish they are after,
fish—and get them.

                    Still I
acknowledge the sea is there and
I admire its profundity only
what does that amount to?
Love also may be deep, deep
as thought, deeper than thought
and as sequential—

                    thought
full of detail, let us say, as
the courts are full of law
and the sea, weeds and
as murmurous: that does not
alter the case either. Yet you
are right in the end: law
often decides cases. Well?
I prefer to go back to my cases
at the hospital.

Say I am less an artist
than a spadeworker but one
who has no aversion to taking
his spade to the head
of any who would derrogate
his performance in the craft.

You were kind to be at such
pains with me and—thanks
for the view.

Ol' Bunk's Band

These are men! the gaunt, unfore-
    sold, the vocal,
blatant, Stand up, stand up! the
    slap of a bass-string.
Pick, ping! The horn, the
    hollow horn
long drawn out, a hound deep
    tone—
Choking, choking! while the
    treble reed
races—alone, ripples, screams
    slow to fast—
to second to first! These are men!

Drum, drum, drum, drum, drum
    drum, drum! the
ancient cry, escaping crapulence
    eats through
transcendent—torn, tears, term
    town, tense,
turns and back off whole, leaps
    up, stomps down,
rips through! These are men
    beneath
whose force the melody limps—
    to
proclaim, proclaims—Run and
    lie down,
in slow measures, to rest and
    not never
need no more! These are men!
    Men!

Lear

When the world takes over for us
and the storm in the trees
replaces our brittle consciences
(like ships, female to all seas)
when the few last yellow leaves
stand out like flags on tossed ships
at anchor—our minds are rested

Yesterday we sweated and dreamed
or sweated in our dreams walking
at a loss through the bulk of figures
that appeared solid, men or women,
but as we approached down the paved
corridor melted—Was it I?—like
smoke from bonfires blowing away

Today the storm, inescapable, has
taken the scene and we return
our hearts to it, however made, made
wives by it and though we secure
ourselves for a dry skin from the drench
of its passionate approaches we
yield and are made quiet by its fury

Pitiful Lear, not even you could
out-shout the storm—to make a fool
cry! Wife to its power might you not
better have yielded earlier? as on ships
facing the seas were carried once
the figures of women at repose to
signify the strength of the waves' lash.

A Unison

The grass is very green, my friend,
and tousled, like the head of—
your grandson, yes? And the mountain,
the mountain we climbed
twenty years since for the last
time (I write this thinking
of you) is saw-horned as then
upon the sky's edge—an old barn
is peaked there also, fatefully,
against the sky. And there it is
and we can't shift it or change
it or parse it or alter it
in any way. *Listen! Do you not hear
them? the singing?* There it is and
we'd better acknowledge it and
write it down, not otherwise.
Not twist the words to mean
what we should have said but to mean
—what cannot be escaped: the
mountain riding the afternoon as
it does, the grass matted green,
green underfoot and the air—
rotten wood. *Hear! Hear them!
the Undying.* The hill slopes away,
then rises in the middleground,
you remember, with a grove of gnarled
maples centering the bare pasture,
sacred, surely—for what reason?
I cannot say? Idyllic!
a shrine cinctured there by
the trees, a certainty of music!
a unison and a dance, joined
at this death's festival: Something

of a shed snake's skin, the beginning
goldenrod. Or, best, a white stone,
you have seen it: *Mathilda Maria
Fox*—and near the ground's lip,
all but undecipherable, *Aet Suae
Anno 9*—still there, the grass
dripping of last night's rain—and
welcome! The thin air, the near,
clear brook water!—and could not,
and died, unable; to escape
what the air and the wet grass—
through which, tomorrow, bejeweled,
the great sun will rise—the
unchanging mountains, forced on them—
and they received, willingly!
Stones, stones of a difference
joining the others, at pace. *Hear!
Hear the unison of their voices. . . .*

The Quality of Heaven

Without other cost than breath
and the poor soul,
carried in the cage of the ribs,
chirping shrilly

I walked in the garden. The
garden smelled of roses.
The lilies' green throats opened
to yellow trumpets

that craved no sound and the rain
was fresh in my face,
the air a sweet breath.

                        Yesterday
the heat was oppressive

dust clogged the leaves' green
and bees from
the near hive, parched, drank,
overeager, at

the birdbath and were drowned there.
Others replaced them
from which the birds were
frightened.
            —the fleece-light air!

The Province

> The figure
> of tall
> white grass
> by the cinder-bank
> keeps its alignment
> faultlessly.
> Moves!
> in the brilliant
> channels
> of the wind
>
> Shines!
> its polished
> shafts
> and feathered
> fronds
> ensconced there
> colorless
> beyond all feeling
>
> This is
> the principle
> of the godly,
> fluted, a
> statue
> tall and pale
>
> —lifeless
> save only in
> beauty,
> the kernel
> of all seeking,
> the eternal

The Injury

From this hospital bed
I can hear an engine
breathing—somewhere
      in the night:

—Soft coal, soft coal,
      soft coal!

And I know it is men
      breathing
shoveling, resting—

—Go about it
the slow way, if you can
find any way—
         Christ!
who's a bastard?
         —quit
and quit shoveling.

A man breathing
      and it quiets and
the puff of steady
work begins
      slowly: Chug.
Chug. Chug. Chug. . . .
      fading off.
Enough coal at least
      for this small job

      Soft! Soft!
—enough for one small
engine, enough for that.

A man shoveling
working and not lying here
          in this
hospital bed—powerless
—with the white-throat
          calling in the
poplars before dawn, his
faint flute-call,
triple tongued, piercing
the shingled curtain
of the new leaves;
          drowned out by
          car wheels
singing now on the rails,
taking the curve,
          slowly,
               a long wail,
high pitched:
          rounding
               the curve—
—the slow way because
(if you can find any way) that is
the only way left now
                    for you.

The Brilliance

Oh sock, sock, sock!
brief but persistent.
Emulate the gnat
or a tree's leaves
that are not the tree
but mass to shape it.
Finis! Finish
and get out of this.

The Semblables

The red brick monastery in
the suburbs over against the dust-
hung acreage of the unfinished
and all but subterranean

munitions plant: those high
brick walls behind which at Easter
the little orphans and bastards
in white gowns sing their Latin

responses to the hoary ritual
while frankincense and myrrh
round out the dark chapel making
an enclosed sphere of it

of which they are the worm:
that cell outside the city beside
the polluted stream and dump
heap, uncomplaining, and the field

of upended stones with a photo
under glass fastened here and there
to one of them near the deeply
carved name to distinguish it:

that trinity of slate gables
the unembellished windows piling
up, the chapel with its round
window between the dormitories

peaked by the bronze belfry
peaked in turn by the cross,
verdegris—faces all silent
that miracle that has burst sexless

from between the carrot rows.
Leafless white birches, their
empty tendrils swaying in
the all but no breeze guard

behind the spiked monastery fence
the sacred statuary. But ranks
of brilliant car-tops row on row
give back in all his glory the

late November sun and hushed
attend, before that tumbled
ground, those sightless walls
and shovelled entrances where no

one but a lonesome cop swinging
his club gives sign, that agony
within where the wrapt machines
are praying. . . .

The Lost Poems (1944-1950)

An Editorial Note

WHEN Dr. Williams first assembled the contents for his *Collected Later Poems*, some poems dating from the period which the collection covers (roughly, 1940 to 1950) were unintentionally omitted. This was chiefly because he had failed to keep, or had misplaced, copies of poems which had been sent out for magazine publication. If we consider the demands on his attention of the "double" life he was leading —a full literary career crammed into the free moments of an active medical practice—it is remarkable that so little important material was temporarily lost. There were also, of course, poems which had been completed but never sent to magazines—pages of typescript that were put aside (perhaps with the thought of further revision) and then neglected, as he became absorbed in newer projects.

In 1953 I began working with Dr. Williams, collecting his letters for the *Selected Letters of William Carlos Williams* (McDowell, Obolensky, 1957). Out of this contact developed a continuing and close association—directed toward a study of his life and work—which has enabled me to examine the papers which Williams has deposited at Buffalo and Yale* and also the literary materials preserved in his home at 9 Ridge Road in Rutherford, New Jersey. In the attic of the house was a huge box in which he had stored copies of the many magazines to which he had contributed. I went carefully through this magic box and also his mother's old iron-bound trunk, containing a copy of *Des Imagistes*.

In the process of examining these repositories I discovered quite a number of unpublished or uncollected (in book

* From 1940 to 1948, Dr. Williams presented a tremendous mass of literary material—handwritten and typewritten scripts; page proofs of books; letters and photographs—to the Lockwood Memorial Library at the University of Buffalo, of which his great friend Charles Abbott was then the Director. During the 1950's he gave an almost equally large collection to the Library of Yale University.

form) poems. Where necessary, I made copies, and, then, at various times, I read and discussed the poems individually with Dr. Williams. Of those which he approved, sixty-one were published in 1957 as "The Lost Poems of William Carlos Williams" in the *New Directions 16* anthology.

17 poems from this group have now been added (pages 253-266) to this new edition of the *Collected Later Poems*, together with other "lost" poems which have since turned up. Further poems from the *New Directions 16* printing (and other sources) will be added to the *Collected Earlier Poems* volume when it is next revised.

Because Dr. Williams did not usually date his manuscript pages as they were written it is not always easy to assign exact dates for their composition. Dates of magazine publication give us clues because he often sent out his most recent work when a request from a magazine editor was received. (This is not to suggest, however, that Williams was a hasty craftsman: in the Buffalo collection there are some poems with as many as a dozen versions; others, like "The Red Wheelbarrow" and "The Yachts" satisfied him in the first draft.) For the tentative dating of certain poems I have had to rely on other evidence—the paper of the manuscript, handwriting, stylistic factors. In 1913, Williams' father-in-law gave him "a ton" of yellow paper which lasted until about 1940. This was supplemented by prescription pads upon which he would jot poems as they sprang out on his medical calls. Later poems were written or typed on two kinds of bond paper, one good, one poor.

Dr. Williams' handwriting was bold and firm until a stroke in 1951 partially paralyzed his right arm, affecting his writing and forcing him to use his left hand for typing. Inconvenient as this was, it did not lessen the quality of his poetry, as the exceedingly high level of the poems of the 1950's indicates. Although Williams made an extraordinary recovery from his first stroke, later strokes obliged him to turn over his medical practice to his son William Eric. The staff of the

Passaic General Hospital, where he had headed pediatrics for many years, presented him with an electric typewriter, and he produced, mostly with his left hand, in this long-dreamed-of leisure, the great poetry of *The Desert Music* (1954), *Journey to Love* (1955), *Paterson V* (1958) and *Pictures from Brueghel* (1962).

Stylistically, a clear-cut change becomes apparent about 1948, as Williams' concern with "American idiom" and the "variable foot" led him to the more formal metric of recent years. The triadic stanzas, which first appear in the poems of *The Desert Music*, are characteristic of this latest period. It is interesting to note how, if we compare, say, "To A Sparrow" (1945—modified free verse) in this volume, with "The Sparrow" in *Journey to Love* (1955—triadic stanzas of variable feet) the metric evolution seems to have affected the substance of the poetry itself. The earlier "Sparrow" is a poetic pastiche, a little sentimental; in the later one, the sparrow (a bird the poet has always loved for its raffish qualities) has become, for him, a specific symbol: [he] "is a poetic truth / more than a natural one. . . . Practical to the end, / it is the poem / of his existence."

JOHN C. THIRLWALL
The City College of New York
September, 1962

The Rare Gist

The young German poked his head
in at the door, handed me
an advertising leaflet for some
drug manufacturer and left,

coloring furiously, after a few
thinly spoken words. My
attention was sharply roused.
It seemed a mind well worth

looking into. And beneath that,
another layer, Phoenix-
like. It was almost, I confess,
as though I envied him

Death

So this is death that I
refuse to rouse and write
but prefer to lie here
half asleep with a mind

not aflame but merely
flickering lacking breath
to fan it—from
the comfortable dark womb

To a Sparrow

Your perch is the branch
and your boudoir the branch also.
The branch, the rough branch!
evergreen boughs closing you about
like ironed curtains
to complete the decor.

The sun pours in
as the roughing wind blows
and who will conceive the luxury,
the rare lightness of
your fluttering toilette like him,
he who is lost and alone in the world?

Princess of the airy kingdoms
the sky is your wardrobe
and yellow roses
the frilled crysanthemums bending
to the late season your park.

Among the clouds your couriers
post to embassies
beyond our fondest dreams
and heaven, the ancient court of saints
whispers to us
among the hemlocks
insistently of you.

To the Dean

What should I say of Henry Miller:
a fantastic true-story of Dijon remembered,
black palaces, warted, on streets
of three levels, tilted, winding through
the full moon and out and
down again, worn-casts of men: Chambertin—
This for a head

The feet riding a ferry
waiting under the river side by side
and between. No body. The feet
dogging the head, the head bombing the feet
while food drops into and
through the severed gullet, makes clouds
and women gabbling and smoking, throwing
lighted butts on carpets in department stores,
sweating and going to it like men

Miller, Miller, Miller, Miller
I like those who like you and dislike
nothing that imitates you, I like
particularly that Black Book with its
red sporran by the Englishman that does you
so much honor. I think we should
all be praising you, you are a very good
influence.

At Kenneth Burke's Place

And "the earth under our feet,"
we say glibly, hating
the "Esoteric" which is not
to be included in our anthologies, the
unthinkable: the younger generation
the colored (unless marketable)
and—Plato was no different—the
"private language."
                          But
the earth also is a "private language"
barring, barring—Well,
principally cash, our one link,
says K. B., with the universal—the
step, the first step out of
domesticity, the familial. Cash. The
first nickel is the first defiance.
But the earth under our feet is
the singing, the winds, the snow—
the surge and slosh of the sea. It's
the indecisive, the rare occurrence
of the expected. The earth
is the esoteric to our dullness,
it opens caves, it distils dews:
the furry root of the fern.
Catalogues are not its business.
Its business, its business is
external to anthologies, outside the
orthodoxy of plotted murders.
                          It is
the green apple smudged with
a sooty life that clings, also,
with the skin: the small green apple
still fast here and there

to the leafless brush of unpruned
twigs sprouting from old knees
and elbows upon the tree
that was cleared of undergrowth about
it and still stands.
        There is a basketful
of them half rotted on the half rotten
bench. Take up one
and bite into it. It is still good
even unusual compared with the usual,
as if a taste long lost and regretted
had in the end, finally,
been brought to life again.

Sunflowers

There's a sort of
multibranched sunflower
blooms hereabouts
when the leaves begin
first to fall. Their
heads lean in the rain
about an old man who,
stumbling a little,
solicitously carries in
his tomatoes from
the fallen vines, green
in one basket and, in
the other shining reds.

Death By Radio
(for F.D.R.)

Suddenly his virtues became universal
We felt the force of his mind
on all fronts, penetrant
to the core of our beings
Our ears struck us speechless
while shameless tears sprang to our eyes
through which we saw
all mankind weeping.

East Coocoo

The innocent locomotive
laboring against the grade
streams its cloud of smoke
above the fallen snow.

Its labors are human to
the superhuman dread that
fastens every mind upon
the coming blast of bombs.

Peacefully we quarrel
over the doctrinal wage-rate,
build the cathedral, split
hairs in internecine wars.

And we too shall die
among the rest and the brave
locomotive stand falling apart
untended for a thousand years.

Rogation Sunday

O let the seeds be planted
and the worry and unrest be invited!
Let that which is to come
of the weather and our own weakness
be accepted!

Let work mate with fertility
the man and the soil join to produce
a world, a world of blade and blossom!
We believe! We believe
in the wonder of continuous revival,
the ritual of the farm.

This is our world and this
is our message to the world and to each other:
Let the seed be planted, the man
and the soil be ploughed equally
by the joy in the planting—
that the grass, the grasses that bear
the seeds: oat, rye and corn
and other yield
speak their message of revival and thrive
by our labor this Maytime.

Coda:

Who shall reap the harvest?
To whom shall the praise be given?
No man—but all men together in love
and devotion. There is no other harvest
and no other praise!
O let the seeds be planted and the rain
and the sun and the moon add their wonder.

The Marriage of Souls

That heat!
That terrible heat
That coldness!
That terrible coldness

Alone!
At the flame's tip
Alone!
In the sparkling crystal

So they stay
Adjacent
Like to like
In terrible isolation

Like to like
In terrible intimacy
Unfused
And unfusing

Threnody

The Christian coin—
embossed with a dove and sword—
is not wasted by war,
rather it thrives on it
and should be tossed
into the sea for the fish
to eye it as it falls
past the clutching fingers
of children—
for them to eye it
and sing, join in a choir
to rival the land and set
coral branches swaying:
Peace, peace to the oceans,
the dread hurricane die,
ice melt at the poles
and sharks be at rest!
as it drops, lost, to its grave.

Translation

There is no distinction in the encounter, Sweet
    there is no grace of perfume
to the rose but from us, which we give it
    by our loving performance.

Love is tasteless but for the delicate turn
    of our caresses. By them
the violet wins its word of love, no mere
    scent but a word spoken,

a unique caress. That is the reason I wake
    before dawn and crush my pillow:
because of the strangeness of that flower
    whose petals hide for me

more than should be spoken, of love
    uniting all flowers beyond
caresses, to disclose that fragrance which is
    Our Mistress whom we serve.

Period Piece: 1834

It was on the old Paterson and
    Hudson R. R.
The first engine out of town
Toot! Toot! blurted the whistle.
    Mc Neill threw
in another scoopful at the door
How's your boy, Jimmy? said
    the fireman
By God, he's a Whistler, son;
I hear the kids are fixing it
    to get married
Let 'em, said his pard. Right!
And that's how the great James
    Mc Neill
Whistler was set up to be born

The Sale

Why should I, who know the cost so well,
Denounce the sale if you contrive to sell?

And why, overriding my extreme objections
Should you, for that, be forfeit my affections?

You are yourself and shall remain so still
And I be I, come world end when it will.

The Counter

My days are burning
My brain is a flower
Hasten flower to bloom
my days are burning

Quietly the flower
opens its petals
My days are burning
My brain is a flower

My brain a flower lost
to its own fragrance
indifferent, idle—
my days are burning

How Bad It Is to Say:

I cannot sing
I cannot sing of cash the king
But I would sing
of cash the king if I could sing
of anything

King cash is got by fear with child
innocence defiled irrational
unreconciled

Christmas 1950

The stores
guarded
by the lynx-eyed
dragon

money
humbly
offer their
flowers.

Kalenchios.
Spanish?
No
they originated

in Germany.
They
bloom so
long!

They're
very easy
to take care of
too

In spring
you
can put them
out

side
and they'll
thrive
there also.

Tribute to Neruda the Collector of Seashells

Now that I am all but blind,
however it came about,
though I can see as well
as anyone—the imagination

has turned inward as happened
to my mother when she
became old: dreams took the
place of sight. Her native

tongue was Spanish which,
of course, she
never forgot. It was the
language also of Neruda the

Chilean poet—who collected
seashells on his
native beaches, until he
had by reputation, the second

largest collection in the
world. Be patient with
him, darling mother, the
changeless beauty of

seashells, like the
sea itself, gave
his lines the variable pitch
which modern verse requires.

Index of Poems by Titles

269

270

273

276